'BRIDGING THE GAP'

G000167818

For David Hope

'BRIDGING

The Christian Sacraments and Human Belonging

THE GAP'

ROGER GRAINGER

sussex
ACADEMIC
PRESS
Brighton • Portland • Toronto

Copyright © Roger Grainger, 2012.

The right of Roger Grainger to be identified as Author of this work has been asserted in accordance with the Copyright, Designs and Patents Act 1988.

2 4 6 8 10 9 7 5 3 1

First published in 2012 by
SUSSEX ACADEMIC PRESS
PO Box 139
Eastbourne BN24 9BP

and in the United States of America by
SUSSEX ACADEMIC PRESS
920 NE 58th Ave   Suite 300
Portland, Oregon 97213-3786

and in Canada by
SUSSEX ACADEMIC PRESS (CANADA)
8000 Bathurst Street, Unit 1, PO Box 30010, Vaughan, Ontario L4J 0C6

All rights reserved. Except for the quotation of short passages for the purposes of criticism and review, no part of this publication may be reproduced, stored in a retrieval system or transmitted in any form or by any means, electronic, mechanical, photocopying, recording or otherwise, without the prior permission of the publisher.

British Library Cataloguing in Publication Data
A CIP catalogue record for this book is available from the British Library.

Library of Congress Cataloging-in-Publication Data
Grainger, Roger.
"Bridging the gap" : the Christian sacraments and human belonging / Roger
    Grainger.
p. cm.
Includes bibliographical references (p.   ) and index.
ISBN 978-1-84519-512-0 (p/b : alk. paper)
    1. Sacraments—Psychology. I. Title.
BV811.3.G73 2012
234'.16—dc23

2011032280

Typeset and designed by Sussex Academic Press, Brighton & Eastbourne.
Printed by TJ International, Padstow, Cornwall.
This book is printed on acid-free paper.

CONTENTS

PREFACE

The Rt Revd Dr Geoffrey Rowell
BISHOP OF GIBRALTAR IN EUROPE

Since the publication of *The Language of the Rite* more than thirty years ago Roger Grainger has been concerned to explore in a number of different ways, including dramatherapy, the centrality of ritual in conveying and enabling human meaning. In this latest book, focussing on the theme of the Christian sacraments and human belonging, Grainger first underlines the fundamental truth that we become the persons that we are in and through our relationships. Belonging (and its counterpart separation) are at the heart of what it is to be human, but belonging and relationship are also challenging to our vulnerability. It is through stories that individuals and communities speak about and establish their identities and draw together present and past. As Grainger writes: religious rituals 'constitute an extended metaphor in the form of a story where meaning is religious; in other words one concerning the relationship between God and people', they 'embody the greatest change of all, within the most fundamentally important of human relationships.'

The late Bishop John V. Taylor wrote a significant book on the life of the Holy Spirit in the Church, with the title *The Go-Between God*. 'Betweenness' is a significant theme in this exploration of the sacraments, in which religious ritual forms 'the turning point around which the tale revolves, the pivot of its action', or as T.S. Eliot put it, 'the still point of the turning world.' Drawing on the work of Van Gennep on rites of passage, Grainger notes how ritual enactment enables the establishment of social identity. The Christian sacraments thus place our individual personal stories, (and the corporate stories of communities) within the definitively larger story of God's sustaining and transforming action towards us and the world which is his creation. Sacraments are where Christians, in Maurice de la

Taille's words, 'place themselves in the order of signs' and do so because in Christ God also placed himself in the order of signs.

In 2003 I was a convenor of a theological consultation on sacraments and sacramentality at St George's House, Windsor, the papers given at which were subsequently published as *The Gestures of God.** In exploring the nature of sacramentality and our contemporary cultural context one of the challenges was how Christian sacramental life could be renewed in a visual age, when it often seemed that non-sacramental churches were the most flourishing. In my presidential address to that consultation I quoted two lines of the Irish poet, W.B. Yeats, in his 'a Prayer for my daughter':

> How but in custom and in ceremony
> Are innocence and beauty born?

Bridging the Gap: The Christian Sacraments and Human Belonging is a valuable contribution in taking these concerns forward, with its setting of what sacraments are about within the wider context of human belonging. It is no less valuable as a theological reflection which is clearly rooted in a long experience of sacramental worship. As Roger Grainger reminds us:

> Everything which is genuinely sacramental is simple: the time, the place, the circumstances. How could it be otherwise when sacrament itself is a breakdown of the arrangements we make in order to create our own world, the ones which we have so carefully constructed for ourselves in our effort to be self-sufficient. If we are to come into God's presence in an honest frame of mind and with a willing heart our action has to be a simple one: to represent ourselves to God, we must rediscover who we really are, and this means depending on the action which made each one of us a person to begin with, in which we abandon the security we were able to make for ourselves and set our hearts and minds on belonging. However hard this may have been, and still is, for us God's love makes it simple enough. The sacraments are demonstrations of this.

Or, as Eliot would have put it, in their depth of enacted meaning they demand 'a condition of complete simplicity costing not less than everything.'

* Continuum, 2004.

This is indeed a book to be read with profit, a book about the gestures of God – the sacraments – which as Newman said 'furnish a mingled argument to the conscience and the imagination,' and which are at the heart of truly transforming worship.

> In broken bread, and wine outpoured
> The meaning of my life is given,
> The sacrifice of love for me,
> God's living bread come down from heaven.

PROLOGUE

As they came near the village to which they were going, he walked ahead as if he were going on. But they urged him strongly, saying, 'Stay with us because it is almost evening and the day is now nearly over.' So he went in to stay with them. When he was at the table he took bread, blessed and broke it and gave it to them. Then their eyes were opened, and they recognized him; and he vanished from their sight. They said to each other, 'Were not our hearts burning while he was talking to us on the road, while he was opening the scriptures to us?'

That same hour they got up and returned to Jerusalem, and they found the eleven and their companions gathered together. They were saying, 'The Lord has risen indeed and he as appeared to Simon.' Then they told what had happened on the road, and how he had been made known to them in the breaking of the bread. (Lk 24:28-35).

CHAPTER

I

DISTANCE AND
RELATIONSHIPS

Psychologically speaking, although each of us is human from birth or even from before that, from the moment of our conception, we do not really become *people* until we are brought face to face with someone whom we recognise as being genuinely other than ourselves. Psychoanalysts refer to this as 'secondary identification,' following Freud's teaching that during the first months of an infant's life she or he experiences what Fairbairn describes as a 'state of identification with the object'[1] – that is with his or her mother – and is consequently unable to achieve the awareness of differentiation from other people upon which what we are accustomed to call human relationships depends. Certainly what we describe as a sense of betweenness as applied to human beings could not exist unless those concerned were identified by each other as separate individuals. It is impossible to reach out to someone, or be reached out to by someone, if the person concerned is simply part of oneself.

Another way of saying this would be to point out that we cannot, by definition, be ourselves if we are unable to distinguish ourselves from other people, and them from us – which is the same process. We certainly need to do this, having cut loose from the self-contained world we previously enjoyed, for from now on we must turn our individual attention to obtaining what we need from the existences around us, and learning to do so on terms which these existences are willing to agree to. The price of gaining our independence is having to surrender this to others in exchange for their dependence upon us.

Being a person, then, involves and depends on the existence, in some way or other, of other persons. The potentialities involved in human-ness depend on our willingness and ability to depend on one another in this way. We do not have to do it; circumstances and our own personal inclinations may make it difficult to do face-to-face; but the closer we draw to this ideal condition of interchange, the more authentically personal we become. 'Salvation,' wrote Charles Williams, 'lies everywhere in interchange';[2] and Martin Buber assures us that 'Man can become whole not in virtue of a relation to himself but only in virtue of a relation to another self.'[3] At a fundamental level, the fear of being alone, cut off from the course of biological existence so that we have to make our own arrangements for living is reduced by the discovery that we are not actually alone; we can form invisible attachments, as many as we can manage, joining in alliance with other vulnerable individuals, gaining a kind of emotional solidarity with them in the knowledge that, just as we need them, so they, too, need us. This is what Paul Tillich refers to as 'The courage to be as a part.'[4] Fear, also, has a part to play within the economy of personhood.

Group belonging, whatever size the group may actually be, whether it consists of three people or three million, both expands and also contracts human-ness. Even the largest group, however, provides opportunities for personal relationships to develop among its members. Sometimes, of course, this happens in defiance of the norms imposed by the structure of the larger group, a situation which carries with it the danger of stigmatization for those who through circumstances or individual choice have created their own, countervailant exercise in group formation. As Major and Eccleston point out, 'Seeking inclusion by others who are similarly stigmatized is likely to have a number of psychological benefits. Affiliation with similarly stigmatized others provides opportunities for self-validation, sharing of experiences, and social support, all of which may help buffer the stigmatized from stigma-based exclusion.'[5]

Stigmatization, along with other kinds of intergroup conflict, is an obvious example of the negative effect of inter-personal solidarity, the social urge to form alliances with people one perceives as being in the same position as oneself; class struggles and political antagonisms resulting in war and revolution are more obvious manifestations of the same principle. The benefits of belonging to a recognizable social, or socio-political group appears to outweigh the disadvantages; isolation and exclusion being more to be feared than having to walk in step with other people – so long as we are allowed to discover ways in which we can go at our own pace. Most people are law-abiding members of some group or other – however much we may proclaim our unwillingness to be seen as conforming in a way which goes against our individuality; and some may gain a more robust sense of self from the enthusiasm with which they assume a recognized group identity as the guarantee of their own individual significance.

Obviously fear plays a crucial part in all this, not only fear of social exclusion, but a more primitive terror of other individuals as such. R. D. Laing, writing in the tradition of existential psychiatry, draws attention to the various ways in which the presence of other people may threaten our hard won sense of existing as authentic individuals, first by dominating us to the extent of treating us as objects rather than people; second by making us feel deprived of any kind of personal initiative, so that whatever we choose to do or be will have absolutely no effect on what actually happens; third, and perhaps the most surprising, by engulfing us in the fury and reality of their loving. To be entirely consumed by someone's love may in fact be, according to Laing, the worst thing of all: 'To be hated is often less disturbing than to be destroyed, as it is felt, through being engulfed with love.'[6]

'As it is felt.' Laing is not impugning love, nor is he describing it as essentially dangerous or destructive; he is simply saying that, existentially, the way we think and feel, we are not always able to deal adequately with its effects. This is particularly the case with small children, but it is also true of those times of emotional crisis in later life when the pressures exerted upon us by psychological changes regarding our own experience of the world and ourselves within it cause us to react in ways reminiscent of childhood, and we feel more vulnerable than we have at other stages in our growth towards full personhood.'[7]

The notion that people are naturally afraid of one another has probably never been popular, even among those who write about human relationships, regarding it as self-evidentially beneficial, and rarely stopping to reflect on the inherent difficulties associated with it, the real problems it presents. At a fundamental level, relationship with other people is never as straightforward as we like to imagine it to be. Even as adults we carry our vulnerability around with us, however skilled we may have become at disguising its presence, a fact which social psychologists have made very clear indeed.[8] Basically speaking, we manage our wariness of others by controlling the amount of distance we locate between ourselves and them. The most obvious example, of course, is to be found in the way we carry out the business of watching various kinds of theatre and drama, making sure that the audience will be physically separated from whatever is going on on-stage (or in the arena or behind the cinema or television screen). These forms of entertainment are the outward demonstration to ourselves and other people of an inward truth regarding the need to be on one's guard against 'getting too involved.'

Getting involved is only one side of the problem, the other side being refused to do so. The dictionary definition of relationship mentions 'the kind of connexion or correspondence or contrast or feeling that prevails between persons or things' (Oxford, 1990). 'Correspondence or contrast:' the two things are actually opposites, even though we find them within the same definition. The reason for this, of course, is that relationship is a polarity. To talk about it as if it were one single thing is to conceal its significance. Relationship is a unity in division, closeness in separation. What it stands for is in fact the action, or process, or movement, or intention of overcoming the polarity which it enshrines within itself.

Certainly, relationship signifies the way we belong together, but we can only do this by overcoming the fear and hostility to which the word itself draws our attention. Our identity as persons depends on this polarity because identity itself depends upon it. In other words, knowing who I am requires an appreciation, as an obvious fact not merely a hypothesis, of who I am not. To return to the theatrical paradigm, I need the space between the acting area and myself in order to permit myself to become involved in the action of the play. Love, forgiveness, grief, despair, joy and renewal exist for me through the separation from whatever it is that is not myself without which I would not be a human being at all.

In order to be persons then, we depend on 'the in-between space we create in dialogue and negotiation with others.'[9] Separation is as vital as belonging because it is on separation that belonging depends; I experience my own selfhood to the degree to which I am able to see

4

myself as distinct from others, which is precisely the degree to which I am able to be in relation to them, the relation that is essential for my own sense of belonging with other human beings. The dramaturgical principle according to which relationships are mediated by the regulation of distance is deeply rooted in human experience. The existentialist philosopher, Søren Kierkegaard, describes how a young actress was able to play Juliet better in later life than she had done when she was the same age as the girl she was playing, the intervening years having given her the perspective needed to become really involved with the part.[10] As Thomas Gray wrote, 'Distance lends enchantment to the view!'

To put it plainly, the 'magic' must have space in which to operate. To be too close is to forfeit our ability to look outside ourselves and leave self-consciousness behind, however briefly, by turning all our attention to something or someone else, thus allowing 'It' to become 'Thou' for us.[11] Certainly this is something we should not regret, because this is what relationship is about – reaching out, leaping the gap which separates us from the rest of creation. It was in fact the distance between actors and audience in Classical Greek theatre which prompted Martin Buber to write about 'the stern over-again-stness of I and Thou' which gave rise to the notion of the unity of feeling that is 'polar' – born of separation.[12]

Polarity, then, belongs to relationship because it represents the aspect of relatedness which distinguishes self from other and prevents us from confusing them. It promotes unity by making confusion impossible. The tendency to homologise is still there, of course, because it is so much safer for us to prefer whatever we are used to, or have grown used to, than having to deal with differences we might not be able to manage and still be ourselves. We use drama because it reminds us of ourselves and the things which happen to us, but is always capable of being dismissed as 'only imagination:' it reminds us very forcibly about our relationships with one another, using real people in order to make the point as strongly as possible – so strongly, in fact, that we need to protect ourselves by keeping the two worlds, ours and theirs, as separate as possible; and by doing so, by keeping their world at a distance, we let it in and allow it to become, at least temporarily, our own. Imagination helps us leap the gap, joining our world to theirs, an experience of closeness and contact which could not happen for us unless the gap existed.[13]

The gap between us protects and encourages. The gap is both safety and potentiality. From the point of view of the dynamics of relationship it is there to be used creatively, not as a way of denying the challenge of otherness but of rising to it. The movement of withdrawal, of refusing to engage with otherness – involving as it does the self's alienation from itself – has the effect of reducing out protective anxiety, our fear of the unknown and untried, and opens us up to an experience which will be authentically new, and to which we find we can really respond.

The action of 'leaping the gap' is a moment of discovery which, metaphorically speaking, liberates us from the chains which bind us to ourselves. It is an experience of personal revelation in which we abandon our habit of analysing who and what we are and move forward into what we are becoming. To identify it as personal puts it in danger of restricting it, as we are used to confusing 'personal' with 'individual,' and this is an experience of belonging with and to something else – a person, a group of people, a thing, time or place involving people, a spiritual presence able to bestow personhood. Our belonging itself depends upon it and we cannot know any kind of human completeness without it.

It is a moment of recognition, when we identify what we have been searching for. If we have not found it, or have found it and lost it again, this is likely to be because we have been looking in the wrong direction, searching in places where it cannot exist – where we have prevented it from working. We have searched for the satisfaction of loving and being loved, as if love, like every thing else in the world which we make for ourselves, were something which could be learned by taking it into ourselves by processes of accommodation and assimilation and thereby growing into it as painlessly as possible. Reaching out to the other across the space which divides us is always perceived at some level or another as a risky, and in some cases actually dangerous, thing to undertake. Its reward comes when we actually manage to do it, when we ourselves make the discovery which beckons us.

In order to belong, yet be ourselves, to *discover ourselves in belonging*, we have to look away from ourselves towards what is unknown and therefore problematic, instead of working away on things already discovered and appropriated in order to improve our position by consolidating it. Genuine belonging will always involve a more adventurous way of relating, one which does not depend on hiding away from challenges or accepting whatever has emerged from the past and simply merging with it . . . For human beings, change must always involve an element of transformation. It is not our enemy, even though it alarms us, since it carries within itself the opportunity to offer ourselves in relationship to whatever it may be that is new for us, and so refresh ourselves in belonging.

Moments of discovery and revelation, *eureka* moments, are surprising by definition. Within the Judaeo-Christian tradition, they are closely associated with religious experience: St Paul is an outstanding example.

> Now as he was going along and approaching Damascus, suddenly a light from heaven flashed around him. He fell to the ground and heard a voice saying to him, 'Saul, Saul, why do you persecute me?' (Ac 9:34)

Mary herself was 'perplexed' by the angel's words and pondered what sort of a greeting this might be. The angel said to her, 'Do not be afraid, Mary, for you have found favour with God' (Lk 1:29,30) and St John records how the revelation of Jesus' true identity at his baptism came as it were 'out of the blue':

> I saw the Spirit descending from heaven like a dove, and it remained on him. I myself did not know him . . . (Jn 1:32,33)

Such things occur as frequently in the Old Testament as they do in the New, which is not surprising as religion itself is definable as a dialectical awareness, in which the human and divine are contrasted in order to be brought into a relationship which is able to have a transforming effect upon humanity. Obviously this is not something which can be appreciated from any other standpoint than religion itself; one has to believe in God in order to be able to make any kind of sense of the idea of his revealing himself like this to men and women and even then this will always be a surprise *because of the contrast*. If the essence of religious awareness is to be found in revelation, God must be allowed to be God. In other words, he must be received as being, in himself that is, very far away: Isaiah puts this very succinctly:

For my thoughts are not your thoughts, nor are my ways your ways, says the Lord. For as the heavens are higher than the earth, so are my ways higher than your ways, and my thoughts than your thoughts. (Is. 55:8,9)

Philosophically speaking religion combines notions of something unknowable from an intellectual point of view with those of an intense personal and social relevance: it is the 'unintelligible-personal.'[14] God is experienced by human beings as higher than heaven and closer than life itself – certainly higher than any thoughts we have about him or any aspirations we entertain to making ourselves as he is. The philosopher-psychologist Karl Jaspers comments that ' There is a particular gratification which comes from a revelation of what actually is.'[15]

And yet the personal nature of the connection, its identity as relationship, abides in the fact that it is necessary for this – literally – inconceivable difference, this immense *distance*, to be overcome in order to for contact to be made – or at least for it to be personal. Some students of human psychology, notably Carl Jung and Viktor Frankl,[16] have postulated a knowledge of God among people which is characteristic of the entire species, although, precisely because it may not be cognitively contained, many members of this species refuse to credit it with any kind of significance. The Christian Church, of course, see this personal relationship as not just present with us but actually presented to us, so that in Jesus Christ we will, quite literally, have something to think about, somebody who, for us, is none other than God Himself: "'Emmanuel,' which means, 'God with us'" (Mt 1:28).

Thus one Testament answers the other in order to bring us into an even more personal relationship with God, an even more secure belonging. 'Even heaven and the highest heaven cannot contain you,' says King Solomon, 'much less this house that I have built' (1 Kgs 8:27); and St John tells us plainly that 'the Word became flesh and lived among us, and we have seen his glory, the glory as of a father's only son, full of grace and truth' (Jn 1:14).

Here there is the reconciliation of all difference in a communion of love, the ultimate Love who is God (1 Jn 4:8). Human awareness is unable to manage a difference as great as this without divine assistance even though difference itself is certainly no stranger to us, being in fact the main way in which we set about making sense of things by thinking round the various phenomena which make up our personal world. It is characteristic of the way we order our existence that so much of our energy should go into the structures we create in order to safeguard the notion of difference, dividing and sub-dividing experiences so that we can avoid situations in which we are faced by the threat of levels of difference which would prove to be overwhelming, something we could not even start to cut down to size, 'engulfed' by a wholeness which defied all attempts to divide it up. When we think about phenomena we naturally use a method of differentiation which, because it depends upon an ordinal scale, always presents us with a hierarchy of values. Any authentic awareness of God throws our scale badly our of true with itself: this is something we cannot possibly begin to 'divide and rule.'

Believers, however, no longer have to wrestle with this problem, having already accepted that attempts to measure God are made totally pointless. God cannot be crept up on in this way. Analysis which we find so useful in the way we normally take our bearings is irrelevant when it come to perceiving what Rudolf Otto called the '*mysterium tremendum*.'[17] The difference is still there, but it is going to need other kinds of resolution than the ones provided by the human intellect alone. 'No one has ever seen God,' says John,

> It is God the only Son, who is close to the Father's heart, who has made him known. (Jn 1:18)

God's way of communicating with us is personal and direct, a matter of experience rather than argument.

Of all religions, Christianity depends most on a person-to-person approach, one in which personhood is exchanged in the way that human relationship itself functions – by imaginative involvement with others and spiritual contact with divinity. Like other world faiths, it communicates by example using the same psychological approach as story-tellers, novelists and playwrights, in which other people's stories are held before us as a way of teaching us how we ourselves should, or should not, think, feel and behave. The stories themselves may be taken to be true (as in the cases of Moses, Elijah, John the Baptist or Jesus Christ), or they may be fiction used to

9

communicate truth, as in Nathan's story about the poor man's lamb (2 Sam 12:1-4) and, notably, Jesus' own parables.

Jesus used stories in order to teach people things they needed to know about themselves: things which constituted this responsibility to God and to themselves. He made no division between these responsibilities. 'The kingdom of heaven is like a landowner who went out early in the morning to hire labourers for his vineyard . . . ' (Mt 20:1). The parable tells how, whatever time of day people began to work, they all received the same pay, an acknowledgement which some of them, the ones who had worked longest, complained of as being unjust. They did this with reason because it was, comparatively speaking, a poor outcome for having endured 'the heat of the sun' for a longer time than the latecomers. *Comparatively speaking* – and human societies are organised according to measurement and comparison. The landowner's assessment of the situation was in line with other 'management guidelines,' those laid down for citizens of the kingdom where love rules, and where the only yard-stick is love.

'Am I not allowed to do what I choose with what belongs to me? Or are you envious because I am generous?' (20:15). What belongs to God is love. Love is his kingdom, and those who belong to it are the ones who are willing to love both God Himself and those whom he loves without having recourse to human criteria for exclusion and inclusion. In the kingdom of heaven there are no politics of belonging because everything belongs to him. This is why 'The last will be first and the first last' (Mt 20:16). The rules according to which in 'the kingdoms of the world' some people are accepted as belonging, while others are rejected, do not apply here. This is not to say there are no rules at all, because the rule of love, as set forth by Jesus himself, is not to be broken: 'I give you a new commandment that you love one another' (Jn 13:34). If for human beings there is a new politics of belonging, this concerns the way we will approach the distances which separate us from one another: are they still to be seen as barriers, or are we able, in accord with Christ's commandment and through the power of his Spirit, to overcome them in the name of him who is three Persons and yet remains One God.

Christians believe that God's loving providence bestows a sense of belonging able to overcome physical distance of any kind whatsoever, even the separation existing between individuals and nations, because of his action in overcoming the meta-physical, spiritual distance

10

which we ourselves have created between ourselves, our entire race, and him: 'I, when I am lifted up from the earth, will draw all people to me' (Jn 12:32). Jesus' words were mirrored by St Paul who describes how Jesus Christ 'Raised us up with him and sealed us with him in the heavenly places' (Eph 2:6). Thus, for followers of Christ, the words of the psalm are abundantly fulfilled:

> God has gone up with a shout, the Lord with the sound of a trumpet.
> (Ps 47:5)

Looked at like this, each Christian sacrament may be seen to stand out as a living parable of human separation and belonging in which the two sides of being a person are reconciled in and through our meeting with Christ. No wonder then that their impact upon us is so powerful, when their significance is so immense.

CHAPTER

II

RELATIONSHIP AND BELONGING

Just as drawing alongside requires having been at a distance and personal relationships involve individuals, so human achievement of any kind happens in the context of purposes which are incomplete and business which remains unfinished. As infants we have to learn how to reach out to people whom we recognise as not in fact ourselves, and find it difficult to do so; likewise, as growing children we need time and opportunity to overcome obstacles which present themselves. Thus, before we can walk we have to learn crawling; in order to ride a bicycle we must put up with falling off at least several times. This is a scenario which goes on repeating itself for the rest of our lives as, even when we are adults and have supposedly 'grown up,' we have to get used to disappointments and failures, to frustration and boredom and occasional feelings of uselessness. One way or another, over the days and years, we accustom ourselves to 'endure the heat of the sun.' 'How many times have I told you? You never seem to learn,' say our parents, and with good reason.

But we do in fact learn all the same and it does take time, more than we expect it to do. Step by step we learn, often – though not always – with a 'little help from our friends.' One of the things we learn is that the difficulties and hazards are actually part of the progress we are making. They are integral to the process of learning, and without them we actually absorb nothing at all, either about ourselves, other people or the world we live in. Just as we need room to reach out, space to relate to whatever is not ourself, so we must have time to learn how to use it. It is another expression of the creative

12

polarity between engagement and isolation that we draw attention to in Chapter I. Just as space implies separation for engagement, so time is travelling in order to arrive. The idea of journeying carries with it both sharing and attachment, a process in which we work in order to fulfil a definite purpose: we 'travel the road to its end.' End, of course, means both 'purpose' and 'destination,' something which the phrase reveals to us without the need for argument or explanation, so that we immediately 'get the picture' of something arduous, even painful, which is obviously worthwhile because it gets us where we recognise that we needed to be. The end of the road is out of sight.

The end of the road is imagined as being unknown in the sense that it is something which may only be imagined rather than fully experienced; where we are now, the road exists, but is 'out of the picture.' The road itself, however, stands for a reality which is ever-present and often burdensome. From time to time the present we find ourselves experiencing is hard to bear, and we make efforts to out-live it by finding ways to relieve the pain it is causing us. This, however, is a time-agony, for the spaces we actually occupy can be changed according to our experience of the moments spent in them. As the Elizabethan poet pointed out, 'Stone walls do not a prison make.'[18]

So far as our experience of it goes, time can be very flexible. When we are not enjoying ourselves, or are bored by whatever is going on around us, it passes slowly and, once something catches our attention and arouses our interest, it appears to move much more rapidly. We tend to be surprised by this, even though we can remember it having happened to us before and, on reflection, have to face the fact that it has always been like this, all our lives. It is, of course, a human phenomenon, one which takes place 'inside' us and does not actually belong to the clock (where hands have suddenly started to go round so much more slowly than they did this morning, when there was such a rush to get everything done in time . . .).

From the point of view of human experience, place and time are the twin factors involved in the way we make sense of whom and what we are, and what we are doing. They govern our natural ways of perceiving ourselves and other people, and the environment in which we 'live, move and have our being,' our world, in fact. Both factors, working together in unison, manifest themselves to us, or are trans-lated by us into, and take the form of a particular story, one in which we ourselves are the principal character. This may appear to be an exceedingly egocentric action on our part, but in order to make sense of anything at all it is necessary to see it in relationship to oneself, and in order to give one's own experience of life – of being *oneself* – any identifiable meaning it must somehow take on the identity, and consequently the signifying power, of story.

Story is our principal way of making sense of life.[19] The present moment gains its intelligibility from its relationship to previous moments, both real and imagined, which are significant because of their own ability to relate both to another and to the wider picture presented by the story of our experience as a whole, which, of course, is what we call 'the story of my life.' From my own point of view, my story is not only something I have but something I can't actually help having. I may use it in a way which is egocentric, reducing everyone else's story to material I am able to include in my own, or I can exchange it with others. When I do this, no longer concentrating on my own past and present but sharing in the world created 'between' persons, our story is returned in a richer and more meaningful way than it was when we forgot ourselves in the moment of meeting.

We need our story in order to discover who we are. At the same time we must abandon our story in order to greet other people and move into theirs. This, as Martin Buber says, is what life is really about: 'All real living is meeting.' I cannot experience the presence of someone else as a participant in my own story without actually going back into myself to do so, but I cannot know them as themselves without quitting the security of myself, my own story, in order to meet them, whether I do this in imagination or actually in the flesh, because it is only by meeting them that I can remember to include them in the way I make sense of my own life. At the same time, my story depends not on the moment of making sense, but on the moment of meeting another person as another, as something, someone, unknown. As Buber says, 'In the act of experience *Thou* is far away.'[20]

Nevertheless, because of this ability to act as a springboard for actual encounter with what is not in fact ourselves, the story is essential. We use story in order to be able to give ourself the opportunity to stand back from events, to extract ourselves, however temporarily, from the succession of events, thereby identifying them as themselves, events with beginnings, endings and time occurring between. We stand back so that we can make a pattern within time by discovering an over-riding purpose in what otherwise would be a baffling confusion. The result is our story about the order in which things have happened to us. Story holds the experiences which over the course of time we have stored away for future use, the things we carry around on our journey because they are still real to us.

These are not things which we have somehow locked away, however. Unless we hold them with us in the present, they decay and become unintelligible. It is our contact with others, involving the interchange between story and story, which keeps them alive. Otherwise they lose their point for us. Sometimes, of course, we find ourselves refusing to make the things which happen to us into recognisable stories because of the pain that would cause us. Psychoanalysts, however, maintain that although we may work hard to do this we only ever appear to succeed in carrying it off so that it is always, theoretically at least, possible to be reminded of what happened to us in those places we have learned never to visit, but which we must do, if our story is to be completed, and its meaning revealed to us.

In the previous chapter we were thinking about the way we use space as a metaphor for relationship. In fact, we also use it as a way of portraying time. In the picture we have of following a road through life, in which we have a trajectory from birth to death, space becomes a metaphor for destiny, our own and that of the human race to which we belong. Doing this together actually binds us closer. The fact that, in this world at least, we are all bound for death is a powerful, if usually unspoken, reason for sharing what we have with other people 'under the same condemnation' as ourselves. In our shared mortality, the passage of time brings home to us the realization that, however individual we may be with regard to personality, biologically speaking we have this one over-riding property in common – that all of us will come to the end of the road which every human being must travel.

In fact this knowledge of death is spoken about implicitly in many ways by the provision we make for the future. 'Don't talk like that,' we say when somebody mentions that the idea of death has started to cross their mind more persistently than it used to do; 'there's no need to go dwelling on it,' we say, in order to protect both them and

15

ourselves from having to face the reality we try so successfully most of the time to avoid thinking about. When we do actually talk about it we use metaphors in order to avoid doing so 'in so many words.' 'Coming to the end of the road' is a useful one, or 'reaching the end of the line,' both ways of getting an idea across about our consciousness of what awaits us all by translating time into space. It is, after all, time not space which concerns us; the space we need is the kind measured in hours or even, perhaps, minutes.

The type of metaphorical expression we use is the story.[21] Stories are extended metaphors which employ people, places, actions and things, with the properties associated with them as mediators of whatever ideas, feelings, or experiences we wish to express – things which are not easy to describe in other ways because, in the absence of any outward form, they have effects which reveal their presence while remaining elusive in themselves. The most common metaphor for human experience over a period of time is that of travelling, or making a personal journey of some kind, 'taking the first step,' or 'moving beyond.' Many extended metaphors describe things happening to somebody, or a group of people, as they progress 'along life's road.' In fact, anthropologists regard the recording of things experienced as belonging together because they happened in succession to the same person or people as paradigmatic of story-telling throughout the world.

A story, then, is a 'slice of life seen on the move.' The movement involved is not always understood as happening on a horizontal plane, because actual physical journeying is taken as symbolic of a spiritual quest. To adapt a phrase of Ursula LeGuin's, we see ourselves as 'voyagers on an inland sea.' Alida Gersie in *Earthtales: story telling in times of change* tells of story as 'The exploration of inner-outer connections.' She goes on to say that, 'Stories are often told in times of crisis and transition in order to provide reassurance and thereby to strengthen the motivation to change.'[22] The awareness of a spiritual journey which runs parallel to the one taking place within the physical world accords with the interchange between time and eternity – a time and time-left-behind, which is clearly communicated by the spatial metaphor. For human beings, the idea of movement for its own sake is both spiritually and psychologically meaningless; to be a journey it must have a destination. The spirituality of story-telling is symbolised by its completeness, for without a recognizable beginning and ending it would not be a story, and could never stand as a metaphor for any goal worth striving for, in this world or any we are capable of imagining.

The conclusion does not have to be an obvious one however. Journeys, whether they are undertaken in real life or in story, do not always reach a satisfying conclusion, or one which appears satisfactory to those taking part. This is particularly so when the search is for enlightenment, and an answer is required which will be final and conclusive. Parsifal's quest does not end with his discovery of the Grail, but only when he has been taught what is required of him in taking on the role of its Keeper. Similarly, in St Matthew's Gospel, the wise men from the East do not arrive at any obviously recognizable destination, and the end of their journeying may be imagined as leaving them with as many unanswered questions as they had when they set out – though, as Eliot points out, not perhaps the same ones: 'This Birth was Hard and bitter agony for us, like Death, our death.'[23]

St Matthew follows this story with an account of Herod's savage butchery of young children, as human selfishness and fear break in upon the course of events with tragic consequences. The bible has many narratives which do not make immediate sense as stories in themselves, but only as episodes in a much wider drama. Revelation happens over time, as well as suddenly, 'out of the blue,' just as dreams must wait for someone to interpret them (Gen 3; Dan 2; Jer 23:28). The story moves at its own speed. Like the narrative concerning the birth of Jesus it runs the gamut of human life in the world, leaving nothing out. Where things are not described, they are implicit; but the fact of human limitation and vulnerability is always a recurrent theme.

To say that breakdown and failure, either intentional or otherwise, are important to the story is an understatement. First, the story being told is God's message to the world about the way he is dealing with sin and disobedience. Second, it is the presence of these things which gives it its form as a story, a record of problems overcome and tragedies survived according to a purpose which has been fulfilled, or one in which eventual victory has finally been assured. This is the way in which we, as human beings, have learned to make sense of life; so it is no surprise that it should be God's way of making sense of a disobedient and intransigent creation. In other words, it is God speaking to us in our own language in stories about people's lives which ring true to us in the light of the knowledge regarding him that we carry within ourselves.

People's lives and their deaths, and the result on other people of their presence in the world are the story of how the divine purpose is worked out through the failures and successes, triumphs and defeats, and in the midst of it all, the sustaining love of God known to us through faith. As the author of the Hebrews puts it:

> Indeed, by faith our ancestors received approval. By faith we understand that the worlds were prepared by the word of God, so that what is seen is made from things that are not visible. (Heb 11:2,3)

The faith of Christians centred upon the cross of Christ, theologically speaking the 'slaughter of the innocents,' links Jesus' birth to his death at Calvary. In this way the whole story is monothematic, centred as it is on the action of the 'Lamb of God who takes away the sin of the world' (Jn 1:29), offering his own life for the world's salvation in answer to the Herod who is sinful mankind, preying on innocence in a time of fear and corruption. Certainly the crucifixion of Christ is the pivotal moment within the Christian story as, with the Son of Man, creation itself is nailed to the cross (Col 2:14). St Paul witnesses to the fact that Christians are baptized into the death of Christ Jesus (Rom 6:3) so that they may be united with him in a resurrection like his (v.5). The cross is our key, too, the heart of our own story which can never be forgotten or overlooked. It is the time of our life and the terms of our belonging.

III

PAST INTO PRESENT

Stories have a beginning, a middle and an end. They concern changes which take place in the lives of the people involved. The middle part of the story is both the end of the beginning and the beginning of the end. Without the end, the story remains unfinished; without a beginning, it cannot function properly as a story because no-one can know what it is about. If it has no middle it can neither begin nor end, nor be a story at all. In fact, it doesn't start to be one until the middle, because it is only at this point that the situation which existed to start with is revealed to us as incapable of development without having to change – and if no change happens it can never be a story at all. In both cases it has finished being a story before it ever started being one. Beginning, middle and end are mutually interdependent.

At the same time if they are to signify a real change they have to be clearly identifiable as before, during and after the time signifying the median position, which is neither before nor after. This remains isolated as 'neither one thing nor the other,' not yet able to move either way without leaving its identity and being swallowed up either by the past or the future, as it exists on the threshold of both. This is the anomalous condition whose purpose is to define past and future by keeping them apart for us, something which is of inestimable importance for any understanding of how change affects out lives.

This is the principal of betweenness, which exists as a function of human belonging in conditions, actions, states of mind, which are 'no longer one thing and yet not another.'[24] As we have seen they are important aspects of human experience because they open us up to the possibility of choosing something new, taking a new direction in life. In the last two chapters we have been looking at the part they

19

play in the way men and women experience both relationships between persons and also events which take place within time. For us the action of encountering another person, when we lose our awareness of ourselves in our discovery, or re-discovery, of them, is the liberation we must have in order to continue being ourselves, being *persons*. We are not conscious of time or of place when we do this or, if we are, they lose any power which they had to preoccupy us. In meeting another we are set free from ourselves so that we may rediscover who we ourselves are. In the Sermon on the Mount, Jesus says that, 'Those who find their life will lose it, and those who lose their life for my sake will find it' (Mt 10:39). When we forget ourselves in the action of meeting, what we find is refreshment and release, as we bestow our own life on someone else.

This then is the principle of life out of death enshrined at the heart of the Christian Gospel in Jesus' own teaching. Jesus himself teaches us in a way that is even more effective in its power to reach us and, having done so, to set about changing our lives. Jesus' own birth, death and resurrection are the living expression of his teaching. When and how he died speaks to us in a way which we find impossible to misunderstand. His story cries out for more than ordinary acknowledgement; it requires our answer. As he gives himself to us, we are to respond by giving ourselves to him. The offer comes from him and takes the form of a life laid down. If we are willing to take it personally we know we should do the same, and the knowledge changes our lives.

It is the story which does this, because we are involved in it on behalf of the person at the centre, who the story is *about*. When we are with him in his story, we lose ourselves in his presence in a way which is able to overcome both place and time, insofar as these dimensions usually affect the way we experience the world we live in. Story itself is able to do this for us. Jesus' story does it more powerfully, more creatively, than any other because it concerns a relationship which already exists between ourselves and him and gives meaning to every experience in our lives. Hearing the story again revives our awareness which we have filed away with other experiences and makes it vivid again.

Stories focus our attention on what is involved in being human. They do this by suspending time and place in order to allow relationship back into our lives as an event to be consciously experienced, not simply taken for granted. When stories are acted this 'event-ness' is dramatically unleashed, by being demonstrated as taking place in our presence by real women and men. Just as stories demonstrate relationship, the life which goes on between and among people shows us how, in the course of their interacting together, their lives are changed. Relationship and change are interdependent. A change in the way we are towards someone else is one which takes place in our relationship to ourselves.

When the story which we are reading or seeing enacted is about our own relationship with God, the change may amount to an experience of transformation. Christians believe that the restoration of the Divine Image in humankind brought about in and through Jesus Christ amounts to the most radical change it is possible to imagine, something which is awe-inspiring even to think about but also something which cries aloud to be celebrated in ways which symbolise the transforming power of the message contained in this story: the message about ourselves and God. In our worship we set out to reflect our experience rather than simply reflecting *on* it. We measure our success in doing so in terms of sincerity and whole-heartedness, not skill; our offering expresses our attempt to respond to the wonder of the story to which we belong.

Religious ritual is the time-honoured way of recognizing transformations. Because their meaning transcends their description, they speak to those who take part in the language of metaphor. They themselves constitute an extended metaphor in the form of a story where meaning is religious; in other words one concerning the relationship between God and people. All stories involve the unexpected – they would not be stories otherwise; all of them describe an important change in the way their characters experience life. Religious rituals embody the greatest change of all, within the most fundamentally important of all relationships.

Where the change happens is between; or rather, it happens in *betweenness*.[25] This is when one way of being has ended and a new one has not yet begun. It is impossible to say if this is the end of a beginning or the beginning of an ending. We may say it is timeless because that is how we experience it. We come to grips with its reality by locating it in story and the enactment of sacred story which is religious ritual and in fact the best way of describing it would be as the turning point around which the tale revolves, the pivot of its action.

The story which is religious ritual balances upon two universes or spheres of being, one divine, the other human, which can only encounter one another in betweenness when each reaches out to the other in the freedom of belonging together in love. Anthropologists who describe religious ritual describe this as liminal experience, by which they mean that it stands at the rite's crossroads, on the threshold ('limen') of the new condition without having left the security of the old one. Since the old rules, which were safe and recognizable, no longer apply, and no dependable new ones have yet emerged, this position is exposed to all kinds of dangers.

Hubert and Mauss[26] led the way for writers like Van Gennep,[27] Bronislaw Malinowski[28] and Victor Turner[29] by describing religious festivals as taking place 'in Eternity.' Turner's is the most vivid description of the timelessness created by the ritual process. Among the Ndembu tribesman whose corporate puberty ceremonies he studied, he writes that, in the middle part of the process the sense of place and time in which the social identity of those taking part depended was suspended, and the conditions of their belonging within the rigidly demarcated community structure temporarily removed, so that instead of coming against one another in the blind antagonism of material interest, 'seeing nothing but themselves,' as it were, they are re-instituted against one another in the transcendent, conscious, recognizable unity of Ndembu society whose principles they are.

Turner is talking here about adolescents, an age group characterised, for reasons of human growth and development, as unlikely to sit tightly to what they perceive to be the *status quo* among their elders. At the mid-part of the ritual designed to ease their way into full membership of the community they are thrown together in a way which, as Turner points out, might well be expected to 'encourage one to follow one's psychobiological urges' (p. 91). Instead, the young people involved develop an entirely different way of relating, characterised by 'an intense comradeship and egalitarianism.'[30]

Turner goes on to say that 'A mystical character is assigned to the sentiment of humankindness in most types of liminality.' The interpersonal nature of the phenomena he is describing is essential to the process of transformation. In addition to inner discord, there must be outer confusion. People are thrown together in circumstances which are likely to increase their distress, separated from their customary

22

way of coping with life, whatever this might be. Put simply, they are thrown together and discover that loving one another is, in circumstances which have been contrived to be as alienating, psychologically and socially, as possible, preferable to living in fear. Not only preferable but now, as a result of having to engage with those circumstances head-on at is were, actually achievable.

The ritual process has the effect of bringing into focus that aspect of relationship which we have characterized as 'betweenness,' in itself a spiritual quality rather than a measurable or quantifiable phenomenon. Turner sees it as the intensification of a familiar characteristic, 'the sentiment of humankindness.' It is however something else which he is describing. Mysticism is never simply an exaggeration of something we are used to feeling. This is why we distinguish it from other more commonplace experiences. Mystical experience breaks in from elsewhere. That is why we find it so disturbing, both intellectually and emotionally, particularly emotionally because we still feel it even when we have succeeded in arguing it out of existence. Turner, and other anthropologists since Emile Durkheim, may regard it as the product of social feeling, but to those involved who are affected by a sense of its presence, it is always more than that, more than and different from . . .

All the same the experience of reaching across to other people gives rise to an awareness of a source of life which in other circumstances is overlooked or ignored. It is as if the action of reaching towards one another manages to unlock a door within us which we may never have known existed or else have forgotten about. What lives beyond the door we do not know and could not say, of course, never having been through it – not *this* door, the one we find opening up for us now. This door is new. One thing is certain, however, and that is that we should not be going through it alone.

Rituals, Clem Gorman wrote, 'lead into higher ground'[31] – not only higher but newer. In the rite, belonging and change go hand-in-hand as, in the company of others, we move into unknown territory. Within the ritual structure this is a place specially set apart for experience of a particular kind involving a heightened sense of personal relationship. It is as if the action of setting apart intensifies our need for engagement both with other people and with ourselves. The young people involved in the Ndembu ceremonies experienced a heightened sense of mutual belonging, despite the considerable physical constraints associated with initiations of this kind. In fact, having to put up with a more than usually rigorous lifestyle seems to have increased their awareness of the importance of values – loyalty, friendship, sympathy with others, simple companionship – which are often overlooked or actually discounted in the competitiveness which characterizes our social lives. Those who choose to spend time on their own in the wilderness bear testimony to the same kind of intensified spiritual awareness, a feeling that although they have turned their backs on ordinary domestic life, they have discovered a way to be more at home in the universe:

> Times of struggle in the wilderness take one to limits, both physically and in the psyche, which one may not encounter in day-to-day living . . . healing the division both within and without.[32]

It is not simply the physical presence of others involved in the same kind of experience as oneself which does this. The action of leaving time and place behind us and setting out into the unknown can bring with it a coming-together of flesh and spirit which is able to transform both ourselves or our world.

Turner's '*communitas*' and Akhurst's 'wilderness experiences' have much in common. Both are radical departures from paths which have become too well-trodden. Each constitutes a conscious journey towards spiritual fulfilment. Only one is explicitly religious, but both may be described as mystical, and involve an experience of belonging. Historians of religion have drawn attention to the function of religious ritual in 're-enacting what has occurred in the past.'[33] Such ceremonies embody the story of humanity expressed through that of a representative figure. In a sense they are all rituals of human re-creation; working at a spiritual level, they affect those taking part in them in a profound way, bringing them closer to one another at the same time, or within the same symbolic dimension, enclosing them more closely with the central figure. 'The process of initiation,' says Mircea Eliade, 'seems to be co-existent with any and every human condition.'[34]

These experiences of 'drawing nearer' are times of physical hardship and spiritual testing. For us they are represented by episodes in Jesus' own story, notably the temptations in the wilderness (Mk 1:12–14; Mt 4:1–11; Lk 4:1–12) and the accounts of his vigil in

Gethsemane (Mk 14:32–42; Mt 26:36–46). Things such as these, along with the trials and tortures, physical and psychological degradations suffered by Jesus, reach their climax in what took place at 'The Place of the Skull' (Jn 19:17), where everything connected with the world of men and women and his own survival as part of it is abandoned. This is the crucial point, the fulcrum on which God's purpose for his world turns.

Christian ritual reproduces the shape of the Christian story. Words and actions which remember Christ's own offering of his own life on our behalf on the cross are ceremonies which celebrate a transformed awareness brought about by an infinitely closer fellowship with God than we are actually capable of imagining, and certainly could not ever think of observing, brought about by Jesus Christ as the expression of his love for his fellow women and men. Working at a spiritual level, these rites hold within themselves the power to move the human soul in the profoundest way, by participating in the transcendence which they symbolize for us. For the believing mind and trusting heart they are the Word which 'became flesh and lived among us' (Jn 1:14). In the sacraments we welcome him home where he belongs, or rather, where we belong *together*. In our ceremonial enactment of the Christian story we are drawn closer to the centre, Jesus Christ himself, whose presence is between and among us.

CHAPTER
IV

SACRED SPACE

The understanding that spaces can have particular significance seems to be as old as the human race itself. These are locations which are defined as qualitatively different from the territory which surrounds them but cannot actually contain them, so that they are not really places at all, but gaps in geography. We locate them by recognising our own inability to tie them down, in much the same way that mathematicians and physicists 'bracket' whatever is currently unknown in order to arrive at a conclusion which will make sense of the phenomena, These spaces are the physical embodiment of our awareness of the demands of a different kind of reality – one which can neither be included, not excluded, comprehended nor ignored. We say that they are symbols of what cannot *really* be expressed, and we leave a space for them. All the same their divinity reaches out to us with a promise of a fullness of being unattainable elsewhere, one which owes its drawing power at least partly to our efforts to keep it under our own control.

Writing in the 20th century, Mircea Eliade[35] summed up the function of places which have been set apart in such a way. To make somewhere sacred involves marking it out as qualitatively different from other places. At the most fundamental level it means imparting significance into the human experience of inconsequentiality, the story which never pauses for us to draw conclusions about its real meaning, but, like an everlasting 'soap opera,' persists in postponing, episode after episode, the moment of revelation. The sacred space uses place to interrupt time, cutting into the homogeneous expanse of human experience, the dramas in which nothing significant or life-changing ever seems to happen, in order to let the light of divine completion in. Every sacred space, says Eliade implies a hierophany, an irruption of the sacred that results in detaching a territory from the surrounding milieu and making it qualitatively different.[36]

Susanna Pendzik puts it like this:

The revelation of a reality of a different order in a given place produces a break in planes, so that the separation is also an elevation.[37]

In the language of religious ceremony, to separate something from something else denotes a change in position within a hierarchy of values. The action of ritualizing is itself a sign of enhancement of intrinsic value. Clem Gorman, as we have seen, spoke succinctly of 'movement into higher ground.'[38] For Christians this sacramental reality is the 'highest ground' of all, so high, in fact, as to be unattainable without the direct intervention of God. The language of religious ritual is the code of human actions of reaching out towards God because it speaks of an ontological rupture in the fabric of human reality, giving rise to a chasm between created and Creator which calls out to be crossed – a wound which, if it is not to prove fatal, must somehow be healed.

The sacred place communicates its message about difference in two ways. First, it sets out to present itself as a special container for divinity, doing so by clearing a space for itself among the distractions of everyday living. Having done this it then proceeds to demonstrate the truth about God through showing us its own obvious failure to fill the space it has made by any efforts of its own. The more intensely it tries, the more obvious it becomes that, although people may clear a space for God, only he can fill it with his life. From time immemorial it has been mankind's experience that the harder we try to close the gap between our own ideas and efforts and the actuality of God, the greater the space between us grows. As King Solomon was to discover, so far as God is concerned, architects and builders turn out to be better at creating distances than capturing and confining essences (I Kgs 8:27).

God calls to us across the difference and uses it to secure our attention. The space is there to be filled, and only He is able to fill it for us. This does not mean we should not try, but only that we should try and fail – and go on failing until we gain the measure of our inability to meet God on any terms other than his own. The purpose of the structures we so painfully erect is to bring home the distance, to underline the presence of a gap in being which it is impossible to bridge by our own strength. They signify the failure of our best efforts to heal a break which can only be repaired from one side. They are not magical spells of any kind aimed at manipulating God into behaving against his will, as so many critics of religion would have us believe, but are much closer to poetry, an attempt to find the right words in the right order, the way of putting things which will best convey what it is that we have to say to God, the things we want to shout across the gap.

The formalised movements and gestures of religious ceremonial, including the order of events within the ritual sequence, signal a different kind of human understanding, a change of attitude towards reality from the one commonly employed to make sense of ordinary life. They envisage a reality pared down to basic principles of being, in which the meaning of what is happening is made clear by the way the rite itself is constructed. Life and death make sense in the way that the rite itself holds together. Its movements and gestures, advances and retreats, acclamations and silences spell out a truthfulness of the human condition with an immediacy which lies beyond the scope of argument. Ritual embodies our religious awareness in living terms, the language of movement and gesture we use to underline things we really mean. Consequently the truth which the rite expresses is truth about ourselves, about who and how we are, and what we need.

The human awareness of an ontological separation from the source of mankind's true identity lies at the heart of religious ritual, which is always a reaching outwards in response to God's call, a movement which is impossible to achieve without God's own action. Whatever its theological reason may be, the distance constitutes our human awareness of separation, on which our relationship with God, like our relationship with one another, always depends. Throughout the world, as throughout history, religious ritual celebrates this difference and calls it sacred, a way of 'leaving room for God' which represents his absence as graphically as it celebrates his presence – the kind of paradox which we associate with poetry, where ambiguity is the main thrust of the message and dramatic juxtaposition reaches deep into our own, personal, life-experience.

Anthropologists have frequently raised the question as to which came first, ritual or drama?[39] The reason why it is difficult to decide, in the absence of any convincing historical evidence, is that both embody the same basic principle. The dynamic of both rite and drama is in the overcoming of distance; both depend on the presence of a distance in order to make the point which they exist in order to make. Martin Buber, for example, looks out across the wide expanse which in Greek amphitheatre separates *theatron* from *skene*, and speaks of the 'polar unity' of feeling which, in theatre, results from the 'the stern over-againstness of I and thou.'[40] It is the facr of separation demonstrated in theatres which draws an audience into the life of the play. Nor is the distance involved one of space alone. We saw earlier how Søren Kierkegaard (also, like Buber, a theatre critic in his early manhood) compares two performances as 'Juliet' given by the same Swedish actress, one when she was a teenager, the other in middle-age, and prefers the later one. The reason he gives is that her performance gained its impact because her increased age allowed her to distance herself from the actuality of youthfulness and concentrate on the idea of being a young girl again. Kierkegaard draws attention to the apparent illogicality of the fact that 'precisely in order to *portray* Juliet it is essential that an actress possess a distance in age from Juliet.'[41]

In fact drama and theatre always depend on some kind of separation of audience and actors. The fascination of theatre, its ability to draw our attention away from out immediate surroundings in order to concentrate on what is happening in the play itself – or in anything which might turn out to be a play – depends on the provision of some kind of distancing mechanism, the most effective of all being an empty space, somewhere where two worlds, that of the audience and the imagined world of the play, can meet and share their experience of meeting. The space exists even before it is filled in any way; as soon as someone enters it the play begins – even though it may be only someone who may (or *may not*) be only a stage-hand.[42] Thus the empty space transforms our experience of all who enter it, whether they do so physically, intellectually or emotionally. As Aristotle points out, in order to be drama, our entrance must first be through our emotions, which break into the act drawing our intellects behind them. Drama and theatre are primarily a matter of emotional involvement.

Or rather, they are the result of a conscious intention on out part to allow ourselves to become involved, what Coleridge describes as 'The willing suspension of disbelief.'[43] This in itself is a cognitive act; we are finally aware of what we have decided to let ourselves in for. As with ritual, we move into a different frame of reference because it is necessary to do so if the truth of the encounter is to show itself among us.

In fact, acting a role in a play is itself a distancing gesture as it safeguards the actor concerned against immediate contact with the audience, while at the same time allowing a personal sharing to take place within the imagined space which is the world of the play. Again the space between exerts its ability to both exclude and include, encourage and dissuade, serving as the necessary go-between in the relationship between actor and role, audience member and the stage personage with which he or she identifies.. We should not assume, of course, that the distance created by a fictional story in itself possesses the same order of significance as that which attaches to transcendence. It is the action of reaching out to another reality, away from one's own, in order to invest oneself in it, which is the same. Drama and story, church building and shrine, written text and liturgy, even extempore prayer, are all jumping-off points, places and gestures specifically set aside for launching out.

In both of the cases we have been considering – religious ceremony and dramatic performance – 'between' is physical, almost measurable, a space to be crossed psychologically in theatres and literally in ritual. In each instance the operation signifies the outward expression of an inner journey, the demonstration of what would otherwise stay out of sight, hidden from view. The voyage which is demonstrated so vividly in ritual and theatre remains implicit wherever people reach out to one another in a spirit of trust. It is the hallmark of what we usually describe as faith in God, and of what such faith entails.

Faith and separation belong together. Certainly faith is belonging but belonging itself takes place within a context of separation. In our deepest movements of soul we acknowledge a distance from God which only faith can remedy. Sacred spaces, places set aside to acknowledge and express our relationship with him, along with the words spoken and actions performed in them, are the outward and visible form of an inward and spiritual mystery – that of the soul's faithful response to the Father who beckons us along the way. The loneliness of the soul would appear to be a characteristic of the human species. For Christians the search for our true home is realized spiritually in the sacraments Our Lord left us, so that through our faith in him we ourselves are welcomed home into the fellowship of Christ.

In the sacraments our faith is made practical. Here the loneliness of single souls is transformed by the companionship of fellow believers toward a common goal. Faith gives rise to faith, as hoping 'against hope' becomes trust in the reality of Christ's presence in the midst of us, to take in the space we has previously left empty and cause it to 'rejoice and blossom as the rose' (Is 35:1). The sacraments reinforce our faith in God's personal love for us as persons who meet to share a common belonging. They speak to us in the language of our life in the world which, through the action and intervention of Christ has taken on an entirely new dimension. Instead of an unacknowledged emptiness, a yearning for wholeness which cannot be satisfied but only disguised, we have an assurance of belonging so convincing that feelings of isolation and separation from God and other people lose all power seriously to threaten our faith. What had so often seemed vague and elusive is now real and personal; such is the experiential force of sacrament.

'Master, we have worked all night but have caught nothing. Yet if you say so I will let down the nets'. (Lk 5:5)

Just like the disciples, we are continually confronted by our failure to carry out the tasks we have to perform. The sacraments keep us afloat on what Matthew Arnold has called the 'sea of faith' by giving us the strength and the courage we would otherwise lack. In the King James Version 'yet if you say so' is simply 'nevertheless.' As such it sums up the quality of Christian faithfulness in a single word. The first Christians hoped vainly for the re-appearance of Christ after his return home to his Father in Heaven. In the meantime they continued about their business setting about building his Church, filling the empty days of waiting with sacramental signs of his continuing presence among them. It is in this way of reacting, this 'nevertheless,' that faith can be seen at work. Like the man who said to Jesus, 'Lord I believe. Help thou my unbelief' (Mk 9:24), Christians are encouraged by the Holy Spirit to 'suspend their disbelief.' For us as for all people everywhere faith requires the presence of doubt in order to be itself, as light depends on, not simply the idea but the actual experience of, darkness. Christ's own cry upon the cross, 'Why have you forsaken me?' (Mt 27:46) lives on at the heart of the inestimable gift he is bestowing on the world he has made by dying on its behalf. This is the action whereby the world is healed of its own self wounding, and human despair is a crucial part of the process. The wound to be healed is nothing less than our separation from God.

The sacraments, then, establish our participation in the action which overcomes the distance between ourselves and our world and the true source – the essential source – of our identity as human beings. In Christ, who is the life of the sacramental, the woundedness which cuts us off from God, has been effectively healed. It is an awareness which we must take to ourselves if our life together is to be genuinely Christian; and it centres on our acceptance of the fact of a separation which only our faith in Jesus can overcome for us.

This book did not set out to be an essay in the nature of religious faith. For Christians, however, it is a subject which may never be simply avoided or kept in abeyance in order to be dealt with elsewhere in greater depth. The aim of this chapter has been to demonstrate, albeit inadequately, the way in which sacramental worship depends entirely on the faith of those taking part, for it is faith in Christ's resurrection alone which can bridge the gap between earth and heaven. Faith is the space which, by Christ's sacramental presence, has for us become sacred.

The sacredness which belongs to sacrament is proclaimed in the world both in the sacramental species, water and bread and wine, and in the setting in which these events take place. Such is the power of these sacramental celebrations that places and buildings, which would otherwise be considered ordinary, can now be regarded as having special religious significance. All the same their significance is tangible evidence of something even more remarkable: the movement of the human soul which, through the action of Christ himself, caused them to be set aside for the fulfilment of a transcendent purpose, that of the world's remaking in the image of Christ. For individuals, baptism constitutes the point of departure from the old way of being and Eucharist the celebration of the new one. Those who remain outside regard these sacred places as doors out of what they identify as the 'real world.' For Christians, however, the place where these services are held are remembered and celebrated as entrances, not exits, for they mark the way into the greatest celebration of all, one which is remembered with joy and amazement, as well as a feeling of the profoundest relief. For such the Christian sacraments are the bridge between one world and another.

The traffic on this bridge moves in both directions. Moving out of this wholeness, back into the world of everyday, we carry its holiness with us. We do so even if we are not aware of it at the time. What has happened to us has been at the deepest level of the soul. It is there that the pledge of our belonging carries out its sacramental work, so that we return again and again to the place of our rebirth in order to bind ourselves closer to the identity bestowed on us. It is this that sustains our souls and directs our bodies in the world which lies on the other side of the sacramental bridge, so that both realities are known to be expressions of the indivisible providence of God, his loving care for all that he has made and in Christ Jesus continues to make (Jn 5:17). We shall go on from here to look at sacraments as symbols of movement, ceremonies which support us on our journey inwards by providing us within the present with a place of spiritual refreshment and refreshment of soul. At these times, in these places, we find ourselves re-discovering our own part in the 'assembling together within God's infinitely compassionate mercy of all the brokenness of the whose creation'.[44]

V

THE MOVEMENT TO HIGHER GROUND

Up to now we have looked at some basic principles of worship in order to discover how they apply to Christian liturgy: distance, story and betweenness, or in other words, separateness, memory and encounter. Reaching across, remembering and meeting the beloved person who calls out to us are all signified by a third characteristic of acts of worship which is the shape of the event itself. We have certainly mentioned this during the preceding chapters because of the important role it plays in the way we make sense of the things which happen to us in our lives. In this chapter, however, we shall be taking a closer look at the way in which rites signify our response or journey towards the God who beckons us.

In religious ritual the conflict which exists in the world of men and women, and the urgency of the need for them to change, is included in the order of a succession of symbolic gestures, which are both physical and spiritual, aimed at drawing us into the presence of the true source of love, peace and acceptance – God, the restorer of all things human. These actions are given the shape of a spiritual journey. Individuals and groups of people set forth upon a voyage into a superior way of existing, acknowledging the human impossibility of what they are all attempting to do and invoking divine help to endure dangers and hardships encountered during their journey, all of this symbolised by the shape which the ritual itself takes. This passage 'through the valley of the shadow of death' (Ps 23:4) represents the ritual form, the journey all human beings make during their lives. To move through it in this symbolic way gives it the particular clarity and emotional impact of a story which those taking part can allow themselves to become identified with, so that it is not simply an abstract idea but an experience, to be lived in the present and remembered in the future. The way in which the ritual-story has been put together conforms to a definite model of human change, the way this is actually achieved rather than just thought about.

The understanding of the part played by enactment in transforming ideas into knowledge is associated with the work of the Dutch anthropologist Arnold Van Gennep.[45] Van Gennep described how corporate rituals associated with the social identity of those taking part, their position within the community, happen in three distinct stages, each one of which was essential to the impact of the whole: the dramatic change which was due to occur at a particular juncture in someone's life, and in terms of the language of the rite was actually taking place now here in the rite itself. The purpose was not to create change but to embody an idea within an experience. Those taking part would be well aware that what was happening to them was intended to be symbolic, and that from the point of view of their ordinary experience of the world these such events could be seen as a 'put-up job.'[46] The way they were put together however made the experience vivid and unforgettable.

Van Gennep referred to these rituals as 'rites of passage.' Two aspects of them stand out. The first is their corporate nature, involving groups of people or entire communities gathered together in order to take part in some way or other within the acting out of the ritual story, thus giving it their own embodied presence. In this way, social reality, actual presence within the community, was the setting for personal change, so that identity and belonging were demonstrated as being interdependent. The second important characteristic is the rite's shape, intended to reproduce the way in which such transformations in identity actually take place. 'A complete scheme of rites of passage theoretically includes pre-liminal rites (rites of separation), liminal rites (rites of transition) and post-liminal rites (rites of incorporation)'[47] This tripartite shape makes the message clear: for genuine change, the current state of affairs must come to an end in order to be regarded as now over. In other words, the present must somehow 'die' so that the future may 'live.' If the first movement of the 'scheme' corresponds to the action of leaving the world of our present experience expressed as a ceremonial act of 'separation,' then the third one will signify the onset of a new kind of existence, and be a 'rite of incorporation.'

Part two, of course, is not so immediately identifiable; or rather, its identity consists in not being capable of being contained in any way. This part of the change process resists attempts to tie it down and make it fit for human purposes. People cannot stay in such a place. Somehow, even if this means moving even deeper into unknown territory, they have to discover a way beyond. The condition has no power of movement in itself and can derive none from either the dead past or the unborn future. It is one hundred per cent threshold, a timeless time and a place without location, necessary to enter and essential to leave behind.

Therein lies ritual's most valuable contribution to life: an ability to take into consideration what is otherwise forgotten or not even actually noticed, the supreme importance of the gap in our thinking when we contemplate change. Ritual reminds us that 'before' and 'after' are not contiguous ways of being so far as our experience of life is concerned although it is easy to think of them that way. Too easy in fact, which is why real life-changes take so long for us. The difficulty is not in adjusting to new conditions once they have started, but in discovering a way to let them start in the first place. Rites of passage leave us in no doubt about the distinction between 'then' and 'eventual' and the pain involved in living through the gap which separates them.

More is involved than wish-fulfilment. Enactments of this kind are ways of reinforcing our sense of reality. Their action in promoting change as it is rather than in the way we usually think about it makes them practical tools for living, as of course does their identity as expressions of a shared belonging. Proclaiming their faith in God's deliverance, those taking part also proclaim their involvement in the lives of one another. They are able to do this because of the ability of the symbol to point in two opposing directions at once, forming a link between opposites – rejection and acceptance, enmity and reconciliation, love and selfishness – things which are so different from each other, so essentially separate that only symbolism can present them as co-existent. Whatever it may be that divides us in our lives as human beings, the rite holds up to God so that we may see it in the light of his conquering love and be empowered to overcome it.

The ritual symbol itself transcends divisions by presenting us with the greatest one of all, that between God and humanity, and revealing it as finally overcome. This rift, says the rite, has been mended, this wound is now healed. And with it, every rift in the fabric or our lives, every wound we have suffered in the course of living out our own personal history. Faith alone can authenticate such a reversal of ordinary experience, and it is our faith which gives life to our religious ceremonies; or rather it is our use of the faith we have been given by God to respond to his call to worship.

In the rites we share, transcendence and symbolism come together, the symbol acting as pledge of the reality which lies beyond its reach. It does this by virtue of being *itself*, the expression of something otherwise inexpressible. Whatever doctrinal evidence may be called on to flesh out its significance for us, the action of making use of it at all shows an understanding of the facts about ourselves which separate us from God and from one another. For Christians, the presence of Jesus of Nazareth, the Word made flesh, represents a reversal of the terms of their relationship with God. It also involves a dramatic change in their attitude towards symbolism – for now the gesture of reaching beyond becomes one of not only reaching but finding. The 'door in heaven' 'stands open for them and our passage through it is in both directions' (Rev 4:1).

Theologically speaking, then, the symbolic representation of a paradox has, in Christ, become the realization of an actual presence. For Christians, symbols of Christ are not tokens of the unseen, but tools for use in the world. This gives our own rites of passage an identity which locates them firmly in the course of events, the times and places which serve human purposes with the revealed will and purpose of God. They are things which we do to remind ourselves of who we are, and so gain the strength and confidence we need to act accordingly. In our ceremonies we proclaim our joy in Christ's gift of himself to us, and show forth our thanks in acts of worship and thanksgiving focused on the symbol which has become our reality.

This mystery is completely practical. In such a functional way the model of the three-fold rite of passage is put to use by Christians 'for building up the body of Christ' (Eph 4:12). Things which are associated with our own vulnerability find an answer within the ritual scenario through our identification with Christ in his death and resurrection. We cannot avoid facts about ourselves which we have to take cognizance of in the course of living our own lives. Involvement in such an experience preserves a psychological realism as well as a theological one. Those who move through the three stages of the ritual process 'with their eyes open' are better equipped for bearing psychological anxieties as well as spiritual pain, not by avoidance but through involvement resulting in a renewal.

Realism is in fact the most outstanding characteristic of a rite of passage. The message is presented in as effective a way as is humanly possible, in other words, by putting it together in three successive stages in order to hammer it home as an event complete within itself, having a starting point, a development and an end. In such a way, we say, the story's purpose was achieved and its ritual enactment carried out. Those involved in ritual believe that the stories which they embody are true, and they express this belief in the way in which they present them. This is the realism which the rite possesses by virtue of being a unique medium of communication, an action proclaiming itself as the truth of an experience by allowing it to stand by itself – as *complete* in itself.[48]

Those who take part in ritual commit themselves to saying what they mean because the rite itself says it for them with a clarity and force beyond their individual power of self-expression. Whatever it may be that they want to say to God regarding themselves and situations in which they are placed is said better from the point of view of the story told by the rite and the conviction with which the rite is able to tell it. This is the rite's particular toughness, that it is put together in a way which carries the stamp of truth, the strength of a well-made human intention. This, the actions whereby we take time, set aside space, and greet one another to share a common belonging come together here to make a statement which bears the stamp of truth.

The corporate worship carried out by Christians illuminates for those taking part the identity of the gospel story with the action chosen to demonstrate its human significance as departure, voyage and arrival, the outline which traces all journeys in time and space. The credal statements which are an essential part of Christian worship deliver their message in precisely the same way as they set out describing the Persons and events which together comprise the faith of Christians: God the Father who gave us life, Jesus Christ who transforms our lives, Holy Spirit who enables us to celebrate, in word and deed, the change which has been brought about for us. The Creeds themselves spell the story out in more detail, but the thrust of the message has the simplicity and completeness that only the three-form shape can bestow. In rite and creed the same story is imaged forth regarding the action of Holy Trinity on the world.

In Christian rites of passage we awaken an immediate awareness of God as He who comes to us to save us, as Jesus came. We set about doing this in the most unambiguous way at our command by re-enacting his story as our own, which he himself has caused it to be, and so proclaiming its transforming presence in our lives. In fact, of course, the command comes from him: 'Do this in memory of me.' This is much more than an ordinary remembering, however, because it calls forth a declaration of assent: 'Yes Lord,' we say, as clearly as we know how, declaring its presence among us as the reality we share.[49]

In rites of passage men and women commit themselves to saying yes as unequivocally as they know how to, something involving each of them as individuals and bringing them all together as one body. What they assent to is their new transformed condition. In Christian terms, it is the change from what St Paul described as 'this body of death' (Rom 7:24) by an action signifying our shared intention to be 'conformed' to Christ's one body (Rom 12:4; 1 Cor 10:17). It is a faithful journey which we must undertake, one where meaning is spiritual rather than literal, but is shown forth and proclaimed in a concrete fashion. Describing this use of the seen to embody the unseen in matters concerning shared belonging, Jean-Yves Hameline writes that:

> The passage from one social position to another is identified with a territorial passage, such as the entrance into a village or a house, the movement from one room into another or the crossing of streets or squares.[50]

Thus profound matters of identity and relationship involving the ways in which human beings are aware of belonging together in the world are demonstrated in the language of time and space which is the *lingua franca* of our creaturely existence.

In rites of passage we draw near to the life we seek in actions which unite the way we think and feel with the things we communicate bodily by means of our ability to vary our physical relationship to whatever or whomever is round about us. We have been summoned to a meeting with an unseen presence and we respond in a way which brings home our own concrete existence in order to communicate, in a very powerful and unmistakable way, the essential difference between sense and transcendence. There must never be any mistake on our part about the distance which subsists between ourselves and the One who calls, in case we confuse his message to us with something we ourselves could invent.

His message to us is clear, lived out among us in the life, death and resurrection of his Son. Our answer needs to be equally clear, so far as we can make it, in unmistakable gestures of understanding and assent which are performed together in the name of God who is Belonging.

CHAPTER
VI

Symbolising Commitment

We have seen that an individual is placed in various sections of society, synchronically and in succession; in order to pass from one category to another to form individuals in other sections he [or she] must submit, from the day of birth to that of death, to ceremonies whose forms often vary but whose function is similar. For groups as well as individuals, life itself means to separate and be re-united, to change form and condition, to die and be re-born.[51]

In rites of passage ordinary, everyday things have received a sacred significance. Being included in the actual story of the relationship between the divine and the human bestows an inalienable holiness, one that is given by the presence at the rite's centre, the person who the rite itself is about, and with whom we enter into an experience of relationship which is able to transform our lives.

This is the purpose of the rite, the intention of those who instituted it. As described here it sounds mechanical, as if the process were automatic, a device for creating a relationship with God which individuals and groups make use of because it works for them and they have decided to continue the practice and reap its benefits. This, however, is to misunderstand the process and so miss the point of allowing ourselves to be involved in it. The point, of course, is the state of mind of the women and men taking part, who believe it will have an effect because they believe in the Presence who inhabits it. They believe this already, which is why they are taking part in the first place.

Rituals like this do not themselves produce faith. They express it on behalf of the people involved, giving them an opportunity to

41

proclaim it in as comprehensive a way as possible taking everything which belongs to the world which they know and understand and offering it to the One who made it. The intention is not to manipulate God in any way, certainly not to bribe him, but to enjoy a close relationship with him by focusing on the action of drawing close to him, carrying with ourselves the human world which is the pledge of our identity, the truth about ourselves. To be included within a ritual scenario symbolising the relationship between God and humanity bestows its own inalienable holiness if undertaken in faith as a response to God's invitation to be transformed by him.

In the rite, people and things are set apart for this sacred purpose, so that they may become representative of the whole profane order, the means whereby that order is transformed by participation in the divine. This is something which the rite communicates by virtue of its use of ordinary human phenomena, the things from which our personal and social worlds are made up, in order to express a divine reality lying outside our grasp. Here an ordinariness is used to communicate truths so extraordinary that they can only be received and understood in the knowledge that it is impossible for us to understand and receive them, in other words, through the ministry of faith (Heb 11:1–3).

With human beings, God is perceived through faith or not at all. This does not mean that traces of him are not be found everywhere in the furniture of the world; otherwise there could be no spiritual symbols. Symbolism of this kind is a way of translating one order of perception into another, standing on the dividing line between worlds and participating in both. Its position 'on the boundary' means it always points in two, or more than two, directions at once. Thus it gives rise to an oscillation between similarity and difference using natural objects and their properties and the human meanings attached to them in order to convey a message about God's invisible and intangible presence for human beings.'[52]

The rite is prosaic so that it may not be dismissed as merely poetry, a technique for expressing things which are true in a sense but have no immediate reality. The ritual experience is both true and immediate. It is rooted in life in order to transform it out of recognition. In order to do so we must surrender to it whole-heartedly, not holding back in any way but giving ourselves to the presence which beckons us. In the ritual process our natural life, with the sense we have of taking part in life so that we are affected by the things which happen to us in it, comes into direct contact with the depth of our experience of the most important thing about our relationship with God. Passage rituals are actions carried out by human beings in order to realise their belonging to God by pledging themselves to him in the way that men and women signify a bond between and among persons, by using what is most recognisable and tangible as the evidence of a real intention to commit themselves to a relationship which is totally new.[53]

The inclusive nature of this commitment is expressed in rites of passage in the sign language of changes which stand for experiences which take place within time and place but transcend the historical events which they re-enact for us. This is essential, because the commitment involved here concerns the revelation of God regarding the entire nature of humankind, all the things which we ourselves have been and done, so that nothing is forgotten, nothing overlooked. The record of our life is contained in the transforming re-enactment, not understated or passed over in any way, but *passed through*, so that the nature of the human-ness revealed in it will stand out in high relief, particularly those aspects of it which draw attention to the pain caused by existing in the world of human experience, in other words, the things about us and our ways of living our lives which stand in most need of transformation.

No act of commitment could stand firm if it ignored these things about us. Rather than simply referring to them, taking them into consideration, it contains this essence. This is the intention of the rite, to present the truth without holding back. We suffer as we are and are changed into what we become. This is the rite's realism, its abandonment of special pleading on our part, any pretence of our ability to stand in the presence of God. As human beings we would prefer not to concentrate our attention on our mortality in so direct and uncompromising a way. Rites of passage, however, being home to us our position.

In the rite we stand in the presence of God. We are willing to do so because we are assured of someone else whose acceptability on our behalf is the token and pledge of our own acceptance. Even though passage rituals are usually public events it should not be assumed that they depend for their meaning on the sheer weight of numbers. The rite's action is personal and cannot be generalised. However many people are involved in the event, what happens does so personally. Because it depends upon an action of complete surrender, the strength given in response is an unique transformation, a way of experiencing life which cannot just be the same as something which we can remember happening to us in the same way before. Throwing ourselves into the rite's action we embrace the uniqueness of what is happening to us now, and are not aware of having seen others venture forth in quite the same way, or having ourselves had the same experience before. Once we are willing to pay real attention to it human spirituality reaches beyond self towards the other which is both real and intangible.

The use of rites of passage may suggest a technique for producing a particular outcome much as a scientific procedure results in a repeatable effect. This would be misleading, however. Scientific approaches do not require the presence of faith in order to produce their effects. The rite of passage is very different. It is the human action whereby individual men and women, either on their own or on the part of the group, proclaim their willingness to respond to a summons to bring their own humanity into symbolised union with a person/presence who will accept them as they are and change them to what they will be. The point which needs to be made, of course, is that religious initiations are consistent experiences involving symbolic death and rebirth, but into the dying and rising of someone else. The relational character of these ceremonies is by far the most striking thing about them, as those taking part share in one another's transforming experience. This is not just the rite of change, a 'visual aid' for learning rules of procedure or territory as yet uncharted. What is involved here is a living-*in* and living-*through*. The hardships and ordeals of candidates are not training exercises, but a re-tracing of steps in order to be able to rediscover what is involved in being human – the struggle, frustration and fatigue, the failure to do what is required and feeling of being abandoned, the purpose which leads on, the hope of fulfilment, the reaching after a meaning. Rites of passage use human experience to encourage us in ways of human hoping which have been crowded out and confused by life itself, so that at critical junctures we benefit from being reminded of them as forcibly as we know how.[54]

The rite is not science, nor is it magic. It does not use forces but presences, and these presences are personal. The form is that of a story rather than a blueprint, because this is the way we talk about ourselves and one another, as if we were able to see ourselves 'from the outside' as it were. Story-form does not make things artificial; it simply alters them to make sense for us. Some stories refer to data which is ascertainable in other ways, from other sources. Stories which do not do this must be taken on trust. The ones which take up the heart of the passage rite must be taken in faith. They may refer to things which have happened at some previous time (or *illo tempore*, a former age), but now they are to be kept in memory so that their message may go on being received. Enacting them in dramatic ceremonies serves to ensure the effects of their message are received at a later time in the most practical of ways, by realising it in living experience.

The ceremonies described by Van Gennep were local examples of a practice of religious initiation to be found in many different locations throughout the world.[55] It seems unlikely that these have spread between and among continents in line with what anthropologists have described as 'cultural diffusion'; after all the shape of the ritual movements is exactly the same as that of human argument which introduces an idea, works through it and then proceeds to knock it home. If the aim of the exercise were to say something in as definite a way as possible, presenting it so that the truth it contained could not be gainsaid, then this is the way one would say it. This is the form of speech used to proclaim something which is fundamentally, completely and finally true, true *forever*.

'Tell them you'll do it; tell them you're doing it, and tell them you have done it.' As with schoolteachers, so with those who construct corporate ritual. Something intended to be authentically new, really changed, has to be asserted with genuine conviction. It can still be denied of course and the offer of newness rejected, or even totally discredited, but, even so, people should be allowed to know what it is that they have decided to turn their back on. In the same way when things are not the same as they were, in some later time and place we should have the opportunity to change in a new direction and be allowed to proclaim the fact both to other people and ourselves. At this level of human being it is never too late to change course.

The gesture is real. It is also simple. The complications involved are not ones which belong to assembling the rite itself, but ones concerning the emotional hazard intrinsic to the process of carrying the rite through. Its characteristic feature is its separation into three parts corresponding to a departure, a journeying and an arrival, brought together in succession so that they form a recognizable event, something which stands out as having a beginning, a middle and an end.[56] When the rite is performed this will represent something successfully achieved and properly carried out. It will do this not merely because those involved have been assured that such a thing is likely to happen, that it always does and has happened, and indeed that it must, or at least should, do so, but because they themselves are personally involved in the process of making it happen and are willing to express their own reality in terms of the ritual action in order to make it their own.

Nobody expects this to be easy; but that, after all, is the whole point of the exercise. Changes of such importance require much psychological preparation. We need to know – or at least think we know – what it is that faces us in the new life which we must be prepared for. We must be sure that this revolution in our own personal way of ordering our lives is actually something which we do want to happen, however anxious we may be about it. The rite itself does not make the decision for us; the resolve to break new ground must be there at least in embryo or we will not respond in the way we need to do in order to give the rite permission to act on our behalf – to speak for *us*. The triple hammer-blow of the rite's action is something which by our willingness to take part in the rite we say ourselves. The rite speaks and we speak in it.

Perhaps this is the most vital contribution made by concrete rituals, that of definition. Ideas change very much more easily than lives. Rites of passage present change as a *fait accompli*. In the necessity to say who we are and where it is that we are bound, and to disclose where we have been in the meantime, we set the record straight both for ourselves and for others in an action intended to say everything that can be said about us with regard to our willingness, and openness, to be changed by the things which happen to us. When we use memory in this way we bring our lives into line with our beliefs and the gate of heaven is held open for us.

At the same time, it is a very ordinary thing to be doing because it is so completely natural for us to show our feelings by expressing them in the movements we make. Nothing could be more appropriate for creatures who possess bodies as well as minds and hearts. The meaning in these movements and gestures is clear and unambiguous, however much we try to elaborate them. This is because the truth with which we deal is for others as well as for ourselves. This is one of the reasons why we have set a time and place for sharing it in the most effective, most demanding way we can; for in fact to carry these ceremonies out in the spirit which conceived them is never an easy matter. In the name of a courage able to defeat uncertainty, a belonging which has put exclusiveness to death, we move beyond ourselves by breaking into newness.

It would be unwise to regard these ceremonies as in any way archaic or outmoded. Rites of passage are to be found wherever human commitment is symbolised. They are not always explicitly religious but those who use them do so to express a loyalty and belonging which only expressive acts can communicate. Writing about secular passage rites in 20th and 21st century Berlin, Aechtner records that:

> The German Humanist Association is currently unable to describe their secular humanist 'civil' confirmation without applying religious, or to be more precise, Christian language. The phenomenon is also present with parents and children who have applied to participate in humanistic *Jugendfeier* [Youth festivals]! For some parents, the ritual is posited within a human 'quasi-religion,' or acts analogous to Christian confirmation.[57]

Rites of passage are a fundamental expression of spiritual aspiration even in the most unlikely places. They are everywhere revealed as the language of human belonging.

CHAPTER
VII

RITE AND SACRAMENT

Almighty God, in Christ you make all things new; transform the poverty of our nature by the riches of your grace, and in the renewal of our lives make known your heavenly glory.[58]

From the point of view of the role which they play in the life of the Church and of the individual men and women who belong to it, the sacraments are clearly seen to be rites of passage, according to the everyday usage of the term. That is, they either signify attainment of important stages in someone's life as a member of the Christian church, or they provide support of a vital kind in stages of life. From this point of view four sacraments, Baptism, Confirmation, Ordination and Marriage come into one category, while the remaining, Penance, Healing and Eucharist, belong within the other. In each one of them, however, our intention remains the same: to inhabit the story of Christ's living, dying and rising so that our grief may be his and his glory ours. We do so because he calls us, and not because this is something we 'presume' to do.[59]

There are certainly many ways in which we could describe the effect of this kind of ritual participation: as inspiration, encouragement, restoration, nurture, re-integration. However we approach it, it is a time of growth, undergirding human weakness with an infusion of divine strength. The ceremonies themselves have been constructed by human beings but the truth they embody reaches beyond human ingenuity. Although in some cases they may be considered to be art, they are never works of fiction, for everything done in them by those taking part must be founded on the action of divinity within the ordinary world of our human experience.

The story of Christ made present in the action of participation is the pledge of reconciliation with the Father and the sign of our union with the source of our being. Because of this, they are also the visible pledge of our unity with one another. What we are celebrating is not merely belonging to an abstract idea, or even a theological concept, but an authentic personal experience: *belongingness*. The sacraments actualise the conditions in which the Church exists. This is why in Christian thought the sacraments are held as representing the Church itself which is nothing else than those whom Christ constitutes within it. Thus the corporate worship of the Body of Christ expresses a measure of coherence, a quality of communion more profoundly real than any concordance of ideas and attitudes. We, says St Paul, are Christ's body; he does not say that it is *as if* we are it.

Once the force of such a consummation hits us we are conscious of a primal experience of belonging which makes nonsense of the division between personal and corporate. The rite itself proclaims the interdependence of the two ideas, as it consists in drawing together a focusing upon the One at its centre who liberates each one of us from discrimination and defensiveness and gives us his power to reach out in love to others and, by doing so, to rediscover ourselves. In the sacraments we taste the truth about gaining life by giving it away to others. In the central symbol of the sacrament we recognize the force of Jesus' words about the dangers of 'keeping oneself to oneself' (Lk 17:22).

As rites of *passage*, sacraments deal largely with people's relationship with time. The rite functions by re-actualizing experiences associated with past events. The history referred to in rites of passage is in fact supra-historical. These were not ordinary happenings, and this is not an ordinary kind of remembering. At some points in mankind's history it presents us with evidence regarding a superior reality to the chronological which makes use of time in order to communicate messages about eternity. The relationship created by juxtaposing sacred and mundane time brings home the extraordinary significance of these revelatory events, and their extreme importance for human beings. Put like this such a thing may seem a primitive way of looking at the relationship between God and the world, and that is how anyone who refused to take religion seriously would almost certainly regard it.

For Christians, however, such a way of looking at time is unavoidable, as St John's gospel makes clear (Jn 1). Not only Christians, of course, but human beings in general have understood the course of history to be God's customary mode of communicating with his world. Even if they preferred not to commit themselves, as disdaining this kind of unscientific language, they have found it impossible not to adopt a comparative attitude with regard to the importance of things which happened, in line with their personal scale of values. Religious believers are more objective about their reasons for attributing significance to particular times and places.

So far as Christians are concerned, miraculous events make time itself the vehicle of miracle. The miraculous identity of the sacrament is guaranteed by the understanding that it is the work of God – his intention mediating his presence. Whoever has arranged the movements or composed the words, he himself is the Author. At the same time, however, this is a miracle enacted, as all God' miracles are, in ordinary experience, and achieves its purpose in terms of its origin in the situation existing in the world of ordinary people, places and events. From this point of view sacraments are a different kind of reality, one which is available for us in time and present with us in eternity. Sacraments are present to the senses and beyond them, within the moment and outside it. This is why Christ's life and death and resurrection are not only remembered but recalled.

The liturgy itself is an act of embodiment. Christ is recalled in actions and gestures which recall his presence in a way that words cannot. It is vitally important that the testimony of the body, the physical and psychological organism should be the means of God's involvement in the work – vitally important not because we say so but because he has shown so. In Christ, he has hammered his message home: in Christ-with-us, Christians regard this as a *fact of life*. Incarnation itself is the action which has drawn us into relationship with God and one another in a way which we cannot avoid acknowledging – an event at which we ourselves are actually present, the living experience of God as total love which is God Himself.

Sacrament, then, is God perceived as being at one and the same time immediate and beyond description. This, perhaps, is why he comes to us like this, in the form of the unanalyzable, the reality which gives life by being lived, not simply thought about, which once we have let ourselves come into its presence 'with true heart and mind' we will never forget and cannot find any way of ignoring. As

Jesus himself said, this action of meeting together in our identity as Christians guarantees his presence among us even though he himself remains invisible to us (Matt 18:20). What we do see, however, is one another, and we move among ourselves in mutual love, all belonging to Christ and through Him to the corporate presence who is Christ in the world of people. This, St Paul points out so forcibly, is a present reality as well as a teaching about eternity (Eph 4:13). In our actions within the sacraments this is the fact regarding ourselves which we recall. It is the fact which makes our actions sacramental.

It is not, however, what we always remember. It seems that we tend to remember ideas more readily than actions, particularly when we have allowed actions to be performed without thinking about them, which can certainly be the case even when they are practically necessary or spiritually significant. Instrumental procedures become automatic, and meaningful gestures empty of meaning. In matters of spirit repetition takes the place of recollection, or recollected*ness,* because it requires less emotional and intellectual effort. Gestures meant to show commitment become habitual; we ourselves are not longer fully present, not really engaged. This is the vanity we mean when we talk about 'vain repetition.' Things are repeated over and over again because they are experienced as being empty, so that by themselves they fail to 'add up' to much. The deficit, however, is qualitative rather than quantitative. It was sincerity of heart which the prophets, and Jesus himself, found lacking.[60]

The most important requirement for sacramental worship is that the people concerned should be there, that they should be present bringing all their own personal reality with them, as Jesus Christ brings his. Realism is the core of sacramental worship. It is emotional realism coming from the intensification of meaning, the holism of individual awareness for each of whom the 'veil of the temple' has been torn in two. It is not enough to hear this story; we must participate in its enactment among us. Only when this happens will our lives be changed by it.

In fact, the Gospel is never something which can be listened to and ignored. It can certainly be disobeyed, as we all know to our cost, but we cannot simply pretend we have not heard it and regardlessly go about our business. If we think we can do this, then for one reason or another we have not really been listening. This is not a story which can be overlooked by anyone who has agreed to pay attention to what is being said, even though they may not be in the right frame of mind to take it seriously as applying to themselves in any way, or their way of interpreting the evidence does not allow them to do such a thing. The same is true when it is fleshed-out in sacramental form. In order to receive it we have to accept our own involvement in it, for it is only when we make it our own that we allow it to come alive among us.

Theologically speaking we may regard what we receive as a gift, or as the response to an irresistible invitation. It is certainly not experienced as something which we ourselves have made happen. It is a gift, assuredly, but one that is made on our behalf, so that we ourselves are compelled to the giving of it. If it is true for us, it is also truth *from* us. We must allow ourselves the knowledge that, in Christ, this is our giving. It is something which I do, rather than an operation carried out entirely by God. On the contrary, it is something God is calling me to do, for my own sake and *everybody else's*. This is what is meant by 'sharing in the sacrament.'

Christian rites of passage address this purpose. They serve as training in self-giving and other-receiving, occasions for personal exchange in which love is the currency. They are events which draw us into a closer conscious relationship with God and with one another, God revealed to us as Love as we ourselves are able to receive Him. Rites of passage show us the significance of the love we ourselves know in our daily lives, the love we can recognise and remember in our giving and receiving, suffering and rejoicing, losing in order to find. In this way they make our knowledge of God in Christ operational within our lives. The practical immediacy of this approach to the Christian life is such that it would be hard to imagine a more important way of sharing our hands-on experience of the effect our growth in Christ has upon our developing sense of belonging in community with others. Rites of passage, in the Christian sacramental form, are about the expression of a love that is able to transform our life in the world at every stage of psychological and social development.

For human beings, knowledge of God must involve awareness of our own mortality. Our hearts have always known that if we are to live in love we must somehow die to self. In the rite of Christian passage the message we receive from ourselves, yet succeed in finding ways of avoiding, is spoken by the Lord of Life. The hand held out to rescue us is that of the human being who intervened to take away that fear by putting it to the test, and he invites us to share the knowledge of victory in our own lives. In the last chapter we saw how passage rituals function to signify new stages in the lives of individuals and groups. The use of symbolism to embody the spiritual within the concrete realizes abstractions, as a wished-for state of affairs becomes emotionally present within the experience of taking part. As acted metaphor is used in order to signify a truth about the transcendental destiny of persons – a religious belonging which points to, and involves us in, a way of being which is real and not imaginary, so the metaphysical use of symbolism 'participates in that to which it points.' The awareness mediated by symbol is not vague and indeterminate, as many people seem to believe the word indicates, but real and practical, expressing itself in actions and words which apply directly to the world in which we are living. It is because it describes a reality which does not merely consist of words that language itself is symbolic. When we use words to speak of Jesus, it is the actual Son of God that we mean, and the same is true of the movements and gestures involved in the liturgy.

F. W. Dillistone described how our ability to use symbols allows us to live 'in a new dimension of reality.'[61] We might perhaps see this as the experience of calling to mind what we know exists but cannot immediately lay hands on. If it is something which we want to make direct contact with, the physical action of imaging it within our bodies pin-points it within awareness. It is this kind of symbolic experience, in which we use our bodies to concentrate our minds, which brings past and future into the present moment. The physical action releases a spiritual gesture, something which in the totality of our embodied self-hood we are really doing. In this moment of personal presence the gap between thought and action is closed for us so that we really do what we want, in the full knowledge that we really want it. In this kind of committed gesture of body and soul, word and deed belong together for us.

Not only for us, but for those whom our gesture, falling in with theirs, confirms and reassures as to our presence and, by reflection, theirs also. This kind of reflecting does not involve moving away into oneself, but making oneself known as a living presence, 'putting oneself on the line,' as it were. We do not do this completely of our own accord; we have been summoned to take part. In several places within the Gospel, Jesus instructs others to perform this kind of action (Mt 3:13–15; 8:4; 14:22–25; Lk 17:14; 22:14–20; Jn 13:1–5). The most outstanding examples concern Jesus' own actions at the Last Supper where his own bodily gestures speak to us with a simplicity and force which words themselves can never do. Words may be misinterpreted or explained away in the light of special circumstances. These gestures are not subject to circumstance. Their meaning is either accepted as itself or rejected as unacceptable to those called to be its witnesses.

This is the quality and depth of witness required from participants in sacramental rites of passage. We cannot depend entirely, or even mainly, on ourselves to contribute this. Here, as in every other aspect of life as Christians, we depend on the gift of God's Spirit (1 Tim 4:14; 2 Tim 1:6), given to us 'according to the riches of his grace that he lavished on us' (Eph 1:7). We are called to take part in gestures of affirmation and belonging, which become effective through the merits of Him who calls us into the awareness of his presence among us. It is not something which depends on our own capacity for belonging and our ability to lose ourselves completely in the act of worship, even though this is what we tend to tell ourselves, mistaking spontaneity and self abandonment for faith. Christ himself does this; he it is who is the acceptable offering and ourselves whom he carries with him. In our enthusiasm, he himself is *theos*.

CHAPTER
VIII

LAUNCHING OUT

To summarise what we have been saying so far, all seven sacraments are rites of passage. They are instruments of existential change which employ the symbolism of an encounter between the ultimate and the conditional, time and eternity, being-as-existence and being-itself. This does not mean that they are all the same, although it does suggest a basic structural form which characterises them all. The Christian sacraments, in common with all other rites of passage, are organised around a central moment of change, the symbolic analogue of the moment of creation, the 'timeless time' when the wished-for state of affairs begins to emerge and the old existence is finally left behind. This is the fundamental meaning of every religious ceremony, for all such ceremonies refer men and women directly to God in the understanding that he is willing to be communicated with in this particular kind of way and no human situation can be the same once this event has taken place.

To this extent, then, all seven sacraments have the same shape. Insofar as they conform structurally to the model of ritualised transformations they inevitably resemble one another. Each however is a specific application of this basic model, not only because it covers a particular set of human social and spiritual circumstances existing at a particular time in the present, but also because of a very specific and definite reference to an event or series of events which took place in the past. This being so we are justified in saying that each sacrament originates in an action of Jesus Christ – an action which calls forth a response from men and women in terms of the kind of ritual behaviour which is natural to them because it corresponds to the way in which they organise their perception of the relationship between man and God, and also between man and man. Christians believe that these actions of Christ, and the interactions which they signify, take place in the present, as Christ himself is at work among men here and now, both liturgically in the sacraments themselves, and also universally through his Holy Spirit, who perpetuates the original sacramental action according to which 'the Word became flesh and dwelt among us' (Jn 1).

Each sacrament, then, is like the other sacraments and also different from them, like them with regard to its underlying morphology and religious purpose, and unlike them with regard to its historical origin and particular function in the on-going life of the Church. Thus it is possible, for practical purposes, to distinguish sacraments which concentrate on transcendence from those which stress immanence – a practical division, not a theological one. The difference between the two groups lies in the way in which the basic symbolism of change and aspiration is used. The first group of sacraments – Baptism, Confirmation, Ordination and the Sacrament of Healing – embody a spiritual journey: an existential process which takes place in time is homologised with an essential change happening within the realm of eternal trust and value. These sacraments look forwards and upwards. They 'aspire to the realm above' and are explicitly purposive and goal oriented. They celebrate the onset of newness, regarding the present in terms of what is to come, what is already coming. From this point of view, the other group – Eucharist, Marriage and the Sacrament of Forgiveness – are celebrations of what has even now taken place. They see what is to come as the true form of what is already present so that they contain the present within the future, rather than the future within the present, as is the case with the initiatory sacraments. They look backwards rather than forwards across the sacrificial death of Christ. They stress victory and achievement rather than struggle and sacrifice. They are less urgent than the other sacraments, more of a celebration than an aspiration. There appears, at first sight, to be more mutuality in these sacraments which present men and women as having achieved a relationship with one another and with God. Their social and religious purpose is to stand as post-liminal rites rather than pre-liminal ones, and that is why I have included them under a separate heading.

And yet at a deeper and ultimately more important level the division is a misleading one. The presence of the Cross at the heart of every Christian sacrament makes nonsense of any attempt to divide them up in accordance with their apparent function within society. The self-offering of Christ governs the significance of these 'unitive' sacraments just as it does the sacraments of 'initiation.' They are all liminal rites, or rather they all include all three kinds of ritual – pre-liminal, liminal and post-liminal – within a single unitary and unifying symbolism.[62] Victory and achievement are the dominant motifs of the first group just as movement and aspiration characterise our experience of sacraments of unification and mutuality. Indeed, the most important thing about any Christian sacrament is that it combines past, present and future in this way, balancing immanence and transcendence without reducing the intensity of our experience of either.

A better way of distinguishing among the sacraments is to approach them from the point of view of the distinction between separation, or apartness, and belonging. Sacraments of initiation and healing draw attention to the human experience of attaining admission to a sense of unity and wholeness. They present a state of affairs which is fragmented both inside and outside. Individuals are aware of not having achieved a task or arrived at a destination that will allow them to be included with others who belong to a particular group of people. Because of this they cling to one another in order to actualise the inclusion for which they are yearning.[63]

This is particularly the state of affairs which the Church exists in order to change. It is why all its rites are ceremonies for joining individuals together in communion with one another through the source of all personal wholeness and unity, Christ himself. The 'single-one' – to use Kierkegaard's phrase – is brought back to God the Father through the intervention of his Son. The action is carried out by the Church in its identity as the single indivisible Body of Christ. The alienation of each self, which violates self from its neighbour, is done away with by another Person's gift of Himself to his beloved brother and sister.[64] Christian initiation, whether by Baptism, Confirmation or Ordination, or the exorcism of evil which constitutes the Sacrament of Healing, is always the action of the One in his relationship to the one. An individual is reborn by baptism into the death of Christ, or received as an adult, confessing and contributing member of the Body of Christ, the living Church, able and willing to take responsibility for the terms on which he or she is received into the fellowship, or receives the sacramental grace of Ordination in order to exercise the functions of the historic priesthood. In the Sacrament of Healing, the Church uses its healing gifts, the healing gifts of Christ himself, to rid one of its members of the sickness which affects him and so restore the integrity of the Body. Each of these sacraments regards the individual on which its action is focused as somebody who is very much 'on his own' and who comes forward to be received into unity with others through the gift of union with Another. This is true however many people are baptised, or confirmed, ordained or healed: all see themselves as needing one another's support in the way so vividly described by Victor Turner.[65]

Indeed, Baptism, Confirmation and Ordination are specifically actions by which people are set apart, and rendered both holy themselves and also able, through the priesthood of Christ, to handle holiness. This inestimable privilege comes only as a result of leaving behind one kind of security of belonging – the natural security of membership of the family, tribe or nation and the cultural solidarity of people with similar interests or abilities, or people who are of the same age or sex, or belonging to the same profession and becoming an outsider as far as those people are concerned. The structural principles which constitute the social universe of the un-baptised, unconfirmed or un-ordained are no longer those which define an initiand's awareness. The history of the prophets, and above all the life of Jesus himself, demonstrate the appalling price paid in terms of loneliness and isolation by those individuals who take God's part in the common life of human societies. What is true psychologically and sociologically is expressed most forcefully of all in the language of religious awareness. To be initiated is to cross a dangerous threshold, and to cross it with trepidation, by yourself. In the waters of Baptism each drowns alone, though they rise with Christ.

The 'spectre of the threshold' arises in Jesus' own life on at least three occasions: first of all when he is tempted by Satan in the wilderness; then in the Garden of Gethsemane, when he was left alone by his disciples, who were 'not able to keep awake for one hour,' and shortly afterwards, at the precise moment when their company was most crucial, 'all deserted him and ran away' (Mk 14:37, 50). Finally, the last most desolate agony of all, when one of the two representatives of suffering humanity chosen to accompany him to his final mission rejects him, taunting him with the words which only emphasise his unique loneliness among men, 'Are you not the Messiah? Save yourself and us' (Lk 23:39).

Only one of the two however. We should never forget that the other bandit's reaction was totally different and equally important. His words bear witness to the deep sympathy which springs up among all sorts of people in this particular kind of situation: the liminal solidarity of those who understand that they 'are under the same sentence' and find themselves able to discount every kind of social and personal difference because of the overwhelming importance of this one vital consideration. In their timeless moment, every other barrier between men is removed and relationships undergo the most dramatic reversal. For Christians, this is the moment of the profoundest reversal of all, that carried out for us by Christ on the cross. At the very moment when the Word of God is regarded as a criminal and a lawbreaker, the bandit establishes that Law's fulfilment in the words of Love itself.

Sacraments are epiphanies of belonging. In them, the action of separation, of leaping into the unknown, a condition for which we are unprepared, is answered by engaging with what is new and life-giving and being established in it. Here, journey means both making the connection and strengthening the bond, joining more firmly together, so that we belong even more personally and intimately. Love is not dependent on times and places, but here at the point of faith – what for us is the whole point – we encounter Jesus himself.

The symbol faces in both directions at once.[66] Each sacrament however employs its own signifying element, some of which concentrate attention one way, some another. In Baptism, Confirmation, Ordination and Healing the sign under which transformation is embodied is that of separation; those to be baptised, confirmed, ordained, healed are actually or symbolically set apart from the rest. The imagery concerns dying and involves immersion in a symbolic tomb or anointing for burial. The core signifier is severance. Other sacraments, however, use different tokens to characterise the movement they embody: expressing welcome, mutual support, the exchange of love, a shared meaning, the hand raised in blessing, the exchange of rings and pledges of love. Here, in Eucharist, Marriage and the Sacrament of Forgiveness the symbolism is of joining together, reconciliation, loyalty. Whether the imagery centres upon separation from what has gone before or union with what has now burst forth will depend on the use to which the sacrament is being put; as to whether the stress is to be on breaking new ground or on consolidating the victory of love that has already been achieved, the sacramental action will always express both these things, its nature and purpose being to encompass a transformation. This, then, is the nature of each sacrament as a rite of passage. Each of them is both departure and arrival, so that to identify some as 'initiatory' and others 'unitive' runs the risk of detracting from the fullness of their symbolic function. Water, for instance, represents birth as well as death, and oil is used for the anointing of kings.

CHAPTER
IX

TRAVELLING ONWARDS

The sacraments we have included somewhat ambiguously under the rubric of immanence, are specifically concerned with the strengthening of bonds which already exist. Marriage for instance traditionally takes the form of a post-liminal ceremony which is preceded by an engagement ritual and a liminal period of betrothal, during which those to be married adjust to the prospect of a new kind of relationship and the implications this has for their present way of life. The wedding ceremony itself is when 'the knot is tied,' symbolised in the giving and receiving of rings. Similarly the Sacrament of Forgiveness signifies re-establishment, re-entry to a state of readiness for Eucharist, the sign of being whole-heartedly committed to Christ.

Penance is the sacramental sign of establishing reconciliation. It represents a breach which is healed, standing as the potent sign of a task known to be well done. Herbert McCabe points to the universal prevalence of such ceremonies and the difference between its sacramental and secular forms.

> Just as most communities have an initiation ceremony, but in the case of Christianity baptism is a sacrament, and most groups have a common meal, but the eucharistic meal is a sacrament, so most communities may be expected to have a rite of reconciliation, but for us it is a sacrament.[67]

Sacramental identity gives special meaning to behaviour which would otherwise be characteristic of human values within the sphere of personal and group belonging. All corporate rituals are religious in the broad, non-specific sense intended by Durkheim, as the expres-

61

sion of spiritual awareness associated with belonging to a group where value and significance is felt to be immeasurably greater than any possessed by any individual members comprising it. In contrast, Christian understanding of sacrament is entirely more specific, referring to and involving a more intimate inter-relationship between divinity and humanity than that acted out in the imagery of other religions which use corporate ritual in order to embody their belief systems. For Christians embodiment has an unique meaning, one drawn directly from the belief that God once lived in a body, one which suffered the cross and rose from the grave and that this corporate God retains his bodily life for eternity, manifesting it in sacramental forms, one of which is the corporate faith of Christians.

In the sacraments, the reconciliation which takes place eternally between God and humanity occurs in and through God's humanity and the divinity which he gives to women and men in Christ. It involves every kind of personal reconciling, interior and exterior, and is the realisation of a union lasting always and forever. This is the *anamnesis* at the centre of every sacrament; the sacramental presence of the reality of Christ's death and resurrection brings to mind and heart the pre-existent unity to which the triumph of love has restored us. At every step in our journey through life we are sustained by the experience of 'God in Christ reconciling the world to himself' (2 Cor 5:19).

Christians believe that their own personal involvement with all other Christians is more real, definite and significant for every aspect of their lives because of the shared divinity possessed by the Church in its identity as a 'faith community,' a group of people united with one an other by the solidarity produced by the act of sharing itself. To be a member of a group of people who share ideals and values concerning the most important issues concerning their own and other people's lives has a spiritual effect itself, particularly in circumstances which make it hard to sustain one's own point of view and way of life. In such situations those who feel and think like you yourself are particularly precious because of the support and acceptance they offer you and the emotional release of discovering that you are no longer alone. To belong to a group of people with whom we are able to identity in this personal way makes the group itself very precious indeed, because of the ability such an experience has to penetrate our self-protectiveness, thereby setting free our yearning to exchange love.

No doubt most religions produce this kind of effect on their members. Christianity certainly does, and such feelings are, psychologically speaking, an important part of being Christian. However, when St Peter tells us that we are 'A chosen race, a royal priesthood, a holy nation' (1 Pet 2:9), he is referring to a different quality of belonging together, different from that envisaged by any other religious teaching outside Christian knowledge of God's dealings with the world. If Christians claim a closer, more intimate spiritual involvement with one another than other groups possess, this is because their spirituality does not originate solely within the group itself, but is a gift of God's own Spirit, not simply to inspire but actually to transform the very nature and being of the group itself – in other words, to adapt St Augustine, God became a member of the group, so that the group might be members of God.

Membership of the group, then, has particular meaning for individual Christians. Within the Catholic tradition, the Sacrament of Forgiveness is an encounter which takes place between two human beings. The Church is represented by the single priest who 'hears confessions,' so that the message about forgiveness is delivered by one Christian to another. This is extremely important, of course, because it embodies the vital understanding that the truth concerning personal responsibility is acknowledged through the meeting of individuals. This level of human intimacy is necessary in order to bring home the individual, as well as the corporate, identity of the Body of Christ. The medium by which we represent to ourselves as individuals the intimacy which exists between God and each one of us, the way we actually think about it, is that of a meeting between persons, *between*, not *among*. In practical terms, we open our hearts to someone and are blessed in the healing transaction between us.

Apart from its theological significance this is obviously important at the psychological level, because it brings home to us the truth which it symbolises in terms of the experience we are most familiar with, that of taking account of a fellow human being, someone who will know, at any rate in broad terms, what it is like to be us and yet is most definitely not us, and the difference existing between the two of us is extremely important in terms of a particular situation we both find ourselves involved in. As in marriage, the encounter directs us to a wider involvement than that taking place between two human beings who encounter each other in the course of their own private business. It is in the quality of our encounter with individuals that the germ of our wholeness lies.

This being so, we should see the Sacrament of Forgiveness as indicative of an attitude of mind and heart which is vital for Christians, not that all Christians should attend the sacrament, but that each of them should be aware of the need to give and receive forgiveness as a basic requirement for living, rather than a particularly virtuous way of behaving. The advantage of regarding forgiveness as sacramental is that it draws attention to the origin of our ability to forgive those who have wounded us and to receive forgiveness from those we ourselves have wounded; for this represents the whole meaning of the Gospel. It is for this that Christ died and rose again, that our human lives should participate in God as Love who is between, *exchanged* Love. 'God is Love,' says St John (1 Jn 4:7) and Jesus himself spells out what this means for us in the most practical way: 'Forgive if you have anything against anyone, so that your Father in heaven may also forgive you your trespasses' (Mk 11:25).

With regard to the number of people who are directly involved on any one occasion, this sacrament is, to use Shakespeare's phrase 'cipher to a great accompt.'[68] The corporate nature is invisible but real. Its identity as a rite of passage subsists in its use as a way of renewing an individual's sense of benefiting from her or his membership of the Christian Church by registering the progress she or he is making on the journey of life, regarded here as a pilgrimage undertaken in the company of other Christians, living and dead. This sacrament is a definite assurance of belonging, the cancelling out of the sins dividing us from ourselves, other people and God. In that its medium is the verbal communication of an understanding essential for any real spiritual progress on our part, it is the sacrament for resuming our journey, turning away from ourselves and outward again towards God and our neighbour.

If forgiveness is encouragement to proceed, Eucharist is nourishment for the voyage, continuing nourishment for as long as it may be needed. Where Christ is, there is the relationship between persons which is the community of love. Christians believe that it cannot be otherwise, in the light of what has been revealed regarding God's identity as the Community of the Holy Trinity. Richard of St Victor, who died in 1173, describes the original relationship between persons as the apotheosis of the action of sharing:

for when two persons who mutually love embrace each other with supreme delight in each other's love, then the supreme joy of the first is in intimate love of the second and conversely the excellent joy of the second is in love of the first.

This, however, is only part of the story; for in order for love to be perfect more than two must be involved in its formation, as

when those who love mutually are of such great benevolence that they wish every perfection to be shared, then it is necessary that each with equal desire and for a similar reason seek out someone with whom to share love, and that each devotedly possess such a one, according to the fullness of his power.[69]

'Someone with whom to share love.' To share joy with someone who returns it is not enough; for real love to happen the joy you both have must give joy beyond you both, joy which spreads. For this to happen, three persons are a minimum requirement. True love, Richard points out, is love growing outwards reaching beyond the immediate delight of the two for whom the relationship has sprung to life.

The importance of this for our understanding of the Eucharist cannot be exaggerated. No better example could there be of sharing than a meal among people who love one another; in this case, no dearer demonstration of the dynamics of Holy Trinity. In Eucharist, the One who is human *for* us, both as representative and saviour, takes, breaks and shares Himself among us. Here in the three-fold action of the rite – separation, transition and re-integration – Christ demonstrates the meaning of his work among us in a way which cannot be confused or misinterpreted. This is a paradigm of the terms of human personhood as the single human being becomes a person in the act of giving him – or her – self away in order that other single human beings may do the same for one another. This, the rite says, is the way to share in the Personhood of the God-in-three-Persons.

To ignore the symbolism, and to regard Eucharist as important to us solely because of the Person who was present at it and the circumstances under which it took place, is to ignore what the sacrament demonstrates about the dynamics of our own personhood. In such a way as this, by the taking, breaking and sharing of ourselves as we are, we become ourselves as we should be, that is, as Christ is and we were created to be (Gn 1:27). In the Eucharist Christ shows us how individuals are transformed into communities of people, and that this is not just by thinking about it, imagining it happening, but by giving their well-preserved individuality in the service of others. Such a thing may only be carried through in faith, just as the truth of personhood itself is to be discerned by voyaging into places which are unknown and putting oneself at the mercy of others. From this point of view Eucharist proposes and involves a universe which is totally transformed, completely reversed in fact.

At the same time, the nature of the occasion as a celebration of love and friendship which already exists comes across to us every time we meet together to share a meal among ourselves and must never be ignored. The ordinariness of this meal, its identity as 'part and parcel' of the way we organize our lives is as precious to us, as vital for our knowledge of God's love for us, as is the humanity of Jesus which it embodies. The Eucharist is a sign of human loving as well as divine acceptance.

In the Eucharist the life of an individual person, Jesus Christ, is taken, broken and shared. Theologically speaking Jesus stands for an entire species, men, women and children in every situation in their lives. This, however, is the language of thought rather than embodied experience of his presence. It is the *specificity* of an individual, personal, relationship with him which makes him precious to us, just as it is our understanding that we are not alone in having such a relationship with him which encourages us to see him as a universal presence in the world he was instrumental in making. Obviously, therefore, his individuality is of crucial importance to us. The Jesus we actually know, the Word who seizes our attention, is a specific person, a Hasidic prophet from a Galilean village. Although he is a member of the Jewish people, he has no human authorisation; his Rabbinic status is unofficial and his legal position ambiguous. He is no kind of social citizen but a social outcast, the friend and companion of other outcasts. His words and deeds proclaim him as someone standing over against current social and religious attitudes and practices, seeking – and needing – human companionship but unwilling to collude with the social consensus in its repression of the individual. Cutting across social conformity, he himself represents the individual human being's freedom to acknowledge a wider allegiance. Just as the human truth about God is this particular man, so the message about God which he embodies is about individual choices.

This is the subject-matter of the first part of the Eucharist, in which Jesus the man is identified as the person whose life, death and resurrection are foretold in the Old Testament and described in the Epistle and Gospel. It is our relationship with him as a person that moves us to lay bare the painful secrets of our hearts as we join together to confess our own personal sinfulness and the sins which we, as individuals, have consented to or colluded with. It is as individuals that we agree to say the Creed together. Similarly, it is in the name of the love between each one of us and Jesus that we offer up our prayers to God, commending other selves to Him, through the personhood of Christ. This part of the rite, its pre-liminal movement, brings home the intimacy which is to be taken, broken and shared at the heart of the Eucharist action.

From the life, death and rising again of Jesus, the 'man for others,' the Eucharist moves to the common life of Christ's Mystical Body, in which individual personhood is transformed by sharing, as the single Jesus gives up his organic identity as a separate individual human being in order to take it up again in perfect form as a person living in the fullness of divine love with other persons. He who is himself relationship, freedom, love, distances himself from himself in order to embrace the isolation of the single human person, the member of an alienated race, so that He may transform the isolation of individuals into the relationship of genuine persons.[70]

Incarnation and atonement are thus shown to be the same loving gesture of God in Christ, whose purpose is fulfilled in the transformation of the world through the action of bridging the gap, cancelling out the division between and among human beings, showing it to be the very same as the one they make between themselves and Him. The Eucharist proclaims, initiates and celebrates the restored relationship between God the Father and his human creation manifested in and evidenced by the presence among us of Jesus Christ. In celebrating it we acknowledge that by his belonging among us we ourselves belong to him, and have come home again to the One who made us.

For those whom he foreknew he also predestined to be conformed to the image of his Son, in order that he may be the first-born within a large family. (Rom 8:29)

Eucharist, then, is the family meal of Christians who are engaged in proclaiming their new way of being in the world. In its identity as a rite of passage, the mode of initiation and union are clearly shown to be interdependent realities – for not only is the one an experience leading to the other, but the celebration of the rite itself involves individuals in embracing the unity to which the rite aspires, so that we are at one and the same time introduced to a new reality and established within the same. Both the rite itself, and the life of Christians taking part in it, are events taking place in this world which transform the significance of its meanings and the value and quality of things which belong to it. To use the language in which this world describes itself, this constitutes political action undertaken to create the social organism of God's earthly Kingdom, which is why the world finds it so threatening.

The Eucharist proclaims the terms of our belonging in the world, as strangers and pilgrims who at the same time are essential for the well-being of all who have taken it upon themselves to set their own terms for belonging. This is what Harvey Cox meant when he called the Christian Church a 'cultural exorcist' whose task is to heal society by working on it from the inside outwards.[71] If this is to happen, the way in which women and men relate to one another itself must change. Belonging must involve the exchange of personhood between and among individuals. Instead of tokens of indebtedness which demand to be honoured these must be the giving and receiving of pledges of love. What God has given in and through Christ requires exposure before and within the world.

The task of celebrating love *among* and *between* finds its consummation in the communion-feasts provided for those around Christ's table, to give them the strength they must have to go on journeying together – for this is the sign for which the world itself hungers, the pledge of a perfect belonging. The wonder of Eucharist is that it is both journey and arrival, the earthly truth about human being and also its divine fulfilment. In its identity as rite of passage, this service embodies all that men and women can express about their new life in Christ Jesus, that they are the restored children of the Heavenly

Father and bear the living presence with them on their journeying, a new Ark carried through a transformed desert.

The Eucharist is the sacrament of Christians 'on the move,' which is another way of saying that it represents and creates a newer, more complete personhood. The action of participating together in the One Christ defines and establishes our humanity as individuals who come together in love so that they may live together in common-ness and unity. Eucharist is the sacrament of community because the movement it speaks of takes place between and among, for the formation of communities as well as leading them out beyond themselves. Eucharist movement is *in* the present as well as *for* the future.

Because it embodies movement to establish Christ's Kingdom on earth it stands always for individuals who are joined together in community, who gain an individuality through the personhood exchanged with other individuals. The action of participating in Christ defines and establishes our own personality, a fact to which Christians never cease to bear witness in the way they experience their lives. As we come closer to him we become more truly ourselves, because it is to his wholeness as the man for others to which we are conformed in the sacramental action of gaining and receiving brokenness. True community as the reality of shared personhood can only come into being where individuals are enabled to be themselves, to find themselves in sharing whatever is most valuable to them.

This, of course, involves a particular attitude of mind on their part, or rather disposition of soul. The gesture of self-giving must have been inspired by the impulse of awakened love. From the standpoint of the individuals involved, Eucharist is the sacrament of their personal surrender, in which they express their willingness to dispense with their own treasured effectiveness, donating it to others so that it ceases to be a responsibility, something which must be held onto in order to establish one's own identity in a world which regards ownership as the only way of ensuring personal safety, and is revealed as fulfilment, the blessedness of giving which alone allows us to receive what we need, the gift of life from elsewhere, life over which we have no control, and which we have in no way earned for ourselves.

The Church, as the Eucharistic community, provides a home for the gifts we treasure but only really enjoy when we give them away. As the community which finds grace, through the presence of Christ, to indulge the soul's impulse to share, the integrity of the whole involves that of each member (1 Cor 12:14–31). The strength of personhood received by individuals in each of the sacraments contributes to the life of the whole community, for individuality participates in Eucharist as Eucharist establishes individuals, by realizing the unity of the divine community which is itself the free interchange of selves.

As the sacrament of 'The Common Life in the Body of Christ,'[72] Eucharist refutes once and for all the argument which dominates human thinking about social organisation according to which the individual woman or man is set over against the collectivity, and personal freedom and corporate responsibility are always taken to be antagonists. Perhaps this is inevitable, since we are so used to interpreting individuality itself from an angle which is potentially combative and aims to put up a bold front in the presence of superior numbers. Community is bound to take away our most precious freedom, which is to 'be ourselves,' by which we mean exercising choice regarding the way we think, feel and behave. We cannot possibly do this, we say, if we have to fit in with a whole crowd of other people, all demanding the right to do the same thing, and if, by some amazing chance, they should all agree with us, then where would our precious individuality be?

According to this way of thinking, solidarity with others involves an unacceptable loss of self-hood. This is particularly the case when other people are united by a common loyalty to an ideal which one does not share, a way of valuing life which makes no sense to anyone who looks at it 'from the outside' which, when we think of the situation from this point of view, is precisely where we locate ourselves. Thus, the sacraments may be regarded as evidence of the Church's exclusiveness, its determination to lay rules concerning eligibility. Their purpose, however, is to speak of God's love for us in ways which reveal it at work in the lives of men and women so that they may know at every stage in the journey what it means to belong to one another in the way that God shows them belonging to himself. Sacraments are festivals of belonging which draw us into ever closer communion with other members of God's family wherever they may be. This is the celebration of the new creation in which division has been overcome as the obstacles surrounding our path are opportunities for sharing. By drawing us into its purpose for humanity and making us fellow pilgrims, the Church uses its rites of passage to proclaim itself as the sacrament of belonging.

'Let us eat and celebrate' (Lk 15:23). The Gospel is full of feasts and the one given to celebrate the Prodigal's return has particular significance from a Eucharistic point of view, not least because of the elder son's reaction to his father's open-hearted gestures of welcome, and the assurance which this called forth: 'all that is mine is yours' (v. 31). The parable illustrates the situation existing in a world governed by human notions of fairness. Quite clearly the younger son has forfeited his right to belong in the family and should be treated as the outsider which he himself has chosen to be. The story brings before us a situation with which we ourselves are only too familiar, in which our own personal worlds and the social worlds which we construe among ourselves are sharply divided into 'insiders' and 'outsiders.'

Jesus' parable tells us quite plainly that this is not the case in God's Kingdom, which is more like our idea of a feast than a magistrate's court or employment exchange. Christ invites us to be guests at his Table, to be sharers in the feast our Father has prepared for him and for us, belonging together in the pain and joy of his living and dying among us. Nothing shows this more vividly than this final meal of Christ who draws his disciples into the closest communion which human beings are capable of attaining, a belonging together in which the distance between what is symbolic and what is literal ceases to have meaning, a sacramental unity: *This is my body; this is my blood.* This, says the sacrament, is what belonging means to all who believe.

The message of the Eucharist is that we are not called to join any kind of club, society, or social status, but to respond to God's invitation to the supper given by his Son. Just as there was no prescribed order of precedence governing the seating arrangements on that occasion, neither shall there be with us. We are all called to rejoice with one who takes away our social self-consciousness, and who is willing to accept anyone who is aware of her or his particular need to attend. The invitation is an open one, which means that the occasion should be publicised rather than kept secret, and care should be taken to present it so that no-one should be able to mistake its importance, and the urgency of the message which is enshrined in the way it is carried out.

The message communicated by the nature of the sacrament as a festive meal is about *belonging*. In the Eucharistic feast, celebration and mission are united. The sign of a perfect belonging draws strangers as well as initiates, as it reaches out to all who recognize themselves to be in the need of this quality of sharing. Knowing this, however, is often less agreeable than it should be to those who are already guests, certainly not as welcome as our host would have it be. There are always those who aim to protect the sanctity of the sacrament, by keeping it safe from 'contamination by the secular.' Like the lamp stand which carries the source of light for the house (Mk 4:21, Mt 5:13; Lk 11:3), so the Eucharist discloses Christ's presence within the world to which he belongs. It is the spiritual source of our own belonging, which in practical terms, as well as theological ones, is the strength which binds his Church together. It is experienced 'wherever two or three are gathered together in my name' (Mt 18:20), particularly where his presence is involved sacramentally, using the language of the senses. This is felt with the greatest force in the Eucharist, the feast of souls and bodies which is the apotheosis of our nature as persons. Just as a beacon draws in those who are seeking shelter and the company of other human beings, so this sacrament reaches out to anyone who is rejected by others or estranged from themselves.

However, the Eucharistic action may be used to exclude as well as include us. Its alienating force is in proportion to its power to attract. Such is the case with everything human, or used by human beings, when it comes to our relationships with one another. The more we yearn to belong together with another, the more we suffer when we believe such a thing to be beyond our reach. It is easy for those who feel that they used to belong to regard themselves as permanently cast out – particularly if the message about belonging is as clear and unmistakable as it is here. They will avoid involvement with Eucharist even when drawn to it by memories of belonging. Much depends on our own willingness to understand this 'tragedy of the Feast.'

Openness, joy, celebration, welcome, must be the hallmarks of our approach to celebrating Eucharist. The joy which we ourselves know, the acceptance to which we owe our membership of Christ's Body, must be obvious to everyone, particularly those who feel themselves strangers among us. Eucharist was given for the breaking of bread *together*. In the Acts of the Apostles we are told how those who had become Christians 'devoted themselves to the apostles' teaching and fellowship, to the breaking of bread and to prayers' (Ac 2:42). The breaking of this bread is for sharing so that all may belong.

CHAPTER

X

REACHING OUTWARDS

The urge to express our deepest feelings and most profound thoughts about what it means to us to be human beings naturally makes use of corporate rituals of belonging. We are conscious of allegiance to an idea, a system, in inspirational teacher, a hero or heroine revered for the things they have done for us and other people and we express our allegiance by making our personal gestures in chorus with those made by others whose intentions are the same as our own and who welcome the opportunity to join with us in the symbolism of the one-in-many, when numbers magnify the significance of one common intention, and the effect of the whole is greater than any sum of its parts would be. The symbol focuses both scope and intensity.

The significance of ritual as a way of communicating the force of things too deeply felt to be simply described by ourselves or reported by others, and which reach out for a language able to by-pass consideration of special cases which lessen the impact of what it is that we really want to say, is evident in almost every sphere of human experience: as codes of polite behaviour when we meet on social occasions, as rules of procedure in public assembly, as evidence of membership of a group of people who share a particular interest or have a particular neighbourhood and gather together to celebrate the fact. Some of them are carried out in public, in the open street or market place, others privately, in the absence of anyone with whom they can be shared. Rituals are carried out at every level of human experience, ranging from the self-consciously intimate to the hierarchically organised expression of national and civic identity. In the Christian sacraments our rituals stand for the humanity which is transformed by Spirit's action among us.

How then can we use our sacramental experience, and the profoundly transformative effect this has upon the way we ourselves regard our lives, to bring a post-Christendom society back into that conscious awareness of God's presence which Christ came to reveal among us? How can we share what we ourselves have with those who, when we tell them about it, have no idea what we mean? The fact that, even in a secular society and a determinedly agnostic, or at least a-religious, culture, the sacraments still continue to be found useful for marking important occasions in the lives of individuals and groups of people, whether or not they are valued by those who ask for them because of their explicitly religious significance. Christian congregations are familiar with the rite of playing host to groups of people whom they have never seen before who require their services for the christening of a child, the wedding of a bride and groom, the funeral of a parishoner. These people are welcomed certainly, but they are not expected to return.

All the same, these and other rites of passage perform the function of aligning the biographies of those involved with the life and death story of someone hailed by Christians as Son of God and redeemer of the world. The shape of the rite itself, as well as its employment at times in an individual person's life which they themselves and other people around them recognize as important stages in their own life story, inevitably draws attention to the importance of story as a way of organizing our experience of life. For Christians the two stories, their own and Jesus', are spiritually identified within the symbolism of the event, as indeed they must be if it is to be a sacrament rather than the solemn demonstration of an intent to carry out a strictly human purpose. All the same the stories are brought into alignment, even if they are not recognised by those involved as being related in a way which makes sense in terms of what they consider to be a realistic view of the world. The faith of others, imaged for them in the words and gestures of the rite, serves to reinforce their own intention to move forward in their chosen direction; they have a sense that an important thing is being done in the way that it should be. In the phrase of countless numbers of those who only attend services at significant times in their lives, it is being 'done properly.'

Rites of passage are always to some extent sacramental, at least in intention, because they embody an aspiration towards a different way of being alive than one which currently exists, a superior quality of existence which lies outside our present circumstances. Because they do this in a way which depends upon their capability to love and to share, to live life in the spirit of self-sacrifice on behalf of the people they see themselves as belonging among, their corporate rituals always succeed in realising the spiritual enlargement to which they aspire. The love which they express is strengthened, clarified, focused, refreshed, in the act of expressing it. There is no doubt at all that such an experience is a source of personal renewal because the intensity of emotion aroused by such an exchange of love magnifies the power to love and to care which was already present in those taking part.

The sacrament is more than this, however, even though it builds upon an awareness of love which already exists in the hearts of human beings. For human love to be creative emotion alone is never enough. Just as hearts require comfort, minds search for meaning. Rites of passage address themselves to the significance, in terms of the human spirit, of an individual's own sense of moving through life, helped on their way by relationships with others whose love and friendship has given meaning and purpose to their own lives. Rites of passage are occasions when we are drawn together to celebrate incidents taking place in the life stories of individuals and the individual members of groups, but the impetus which gives rise to them originates in a common sense of belonging together, the same sense which leads committed football supporters to sing, 'You'll never walk alone,' and 'Abide with me.'

Opportunities to celebrate the need to belong together give rise to instances of its open expression. Baptisms, first Communions, Confirmations, Weddings and funerals give rise to powerful feelings even among those who would not otherwise admit to being in any way religious. There are times when the story of God's love for us strikes home because we are willing to allow it to do so because of the way in which it is presented, as the story which alone can make sense of our own.

Sacrament embodies the Being of God within the existence of the human. The vehicle for this is a story, that of the Word made flesh for us, in the setting of our own individual stories. The power of a human narrative to involve its hearers, so that they give themselves to the story in a gesture of self-forgetfulness, a gift to those whom it is about, renders this the most appropriate form of communication between persons. In this case the story is the amazing record of Christ's Incarnation, Crucifixion and Resurrection made present in a symbolic re-enactment moving enough for us to abandon our defences and open our hearts to what it offers. The sacrament is the direct action of God among us and we receive it in and through our own humanity. This is the true human belonging, and sacrament is its pledge. As ways of bringing us closer to the story of Jesus by bringing us into his actual sacramental presence among us, these occasions of rejoicing together are the most personal of all mission strategies. This in the very deepest sense, is evangelism through involvement.

Christian pastoral work reveals a very important fact about life in the 21st century – that those whose minds appear to be firmly closed regarding anything to do with religion nevertheless possess open hearts for other expressions of human spirituality. Edward Bailey[73] argues convincingly that, in a secular society such as this, our aware-ness of the need to feel inspired seizes upon a range of alternative objects of devotion. Sport, music, travel, personal fitness, these and many other areas of life, as well as actual organisations, clubs and institutions such as large business concerns, become 'implicit' reli-gions in order to make up for the failure of 'explicit' religions to present themselves as credible within an intellectual atmosphere which hesitates to give credence to anything regarded as scientifically unascertainable. Religious organisations are real enough, but what they represent cannot be substantiated according to the way we set about proving things nowadays. After all, changed lives may be accounted for in other ways: psychologically, sociologically, medically, or simply as the result of chance.

Looking for somewhere to belong, something to which they can give their hearts, men and women choose an idea, system or organi-sation which they regard as more reliable, by modern standards more accountable than they regard the Church to be. Human spirituality gives its own kind of sacredness to whatever it chooses. As G. K. Chesterton remarked, 'If a man doesn't believe in God, he will believe in anything.' This is not to say, however, that believing in anything will actually satisfy him. It cannot simply be a matter of chance that football crowds, who ostensibly worship at the shrine of a particular team, so wholeheartedly ask God to abide with them. Put on the spot, the majority of people in Great Britain admit to believing in God.

The devotion offered to His rivals is only a respectable disguise for their true feelings in a world which has conspired to refuse to be convinced.

So – who will baptise this submerged longing? How may it be brought to the surface? The answer is with individuals. Immersion in the sacraments leaves its mark upon us in ways which arguments about God's existence can never do. Here, in these actions and intentions, more is accomplished than in brief physical gesture; to bring created things into the present of the Source of Life in this way transforms our attitude towards, *and consequently our experience of*, everything human, including the assumptions we make and the logic on which we depend in order to make sense of things for ourselves. In the sacrament God Himself enters the world we are used to regarding as our own, bracketing our life with Christ's. The world we are used to finds difficulty in making sense of God. Here, in rites of sacramental passage, he makes sense of us.

Looking back over what I have written, I am very conscious of how much as been left unsaid. This must be the case, of course, in any book about the sacraments. In this one I have concentrated my attention on a single idea: that these ceremonies, all of them based upon the story of Jesus and firmly rooted in his teaching, are ways in which we set out to conform our own lives to his. They answer a need which we have to belong to him as he does to us. This is often said; in the sacraments, however, it is *lived out*. Because we know ourselves unable to live as God created us, we use story and symbol, the sacramental reality of Jesus' presence in the circumstances of our own lives – the things we need in order to go on living – to align our intentions to his. Doing this we carry out an urge to present ourselves to God and one another which is characteristic of women and men all over the world at all stages of their lives. Everywhere human beings try to give shape and meaning to the things they share together by bringing them before God, the source of all that is true and meaningful. The action of doing so draws them together and this sense of belonging is itself a symbol that they belong to God. Christians, however, learn to belong at the hand of One who knew its real cost.

It would be impossible to imagine a more personal invitation than this one, which is addressed to an individual human soul. Even this, however, may turn out to be a disadvantage because of the human tendency to regard numbers as the most important consideration, as if the business of bringing in the Kingdom of God were simply a matter of inducing as many people as possible to add their names of those willing to attend. After all, this is the way we carry out our own business, with publicity campaigns and recruitment drives. Success is measured by numbers, with the result that only those personal experiences which can be evaluated in terms of the degree to which they fit in with others of the same kind can claim anything of significance in the eyes of those who ask how they can know something is true unless they can measure it alongside something else.

Present day evangelists and popular preachers gauge their success in terms of the size of the crowds who come to their meetings. Similarly priests and ministers keep checks on the statistics regarding attendance at church services. Sacrament makes size redundant. Or, rather, it renders it paradoxical. The smaller the event, the more force it can have. God is not impressed by size, even though we may be. This is a hard lesson for us to learn; and yet, when we look back on the really important moments in our own lives, we may reflect on how few of these were large scale events, occasions which we ourselves, or others on our behalf, had spent time and effort putting together, and how, in the middle of such occasions, we were suddenly alone, by ourselves with the person who had come to meet us – not because of our skill in stage management but in spite of it.

Everything which is genuinely sacramental is simple: the time, the place, the circumstances. How could it be otherwise when sacrament itself is a breakdown of the arrangements we make in order to create our own worlds, the ones which we have so carefully constructed for ourselves in our effort to be self-sufficient. If we are to come into God's presence in an honest frame of mind and with a willing heart our action has to be a simple one: to present ourselves to God, we must rediscover who we really are, and this means depending on the action which made each one of us a person to begin with, in which we abandon the security we were able to make for ourselves and set our hearts and minds on belonging. However hard this may have been, and still is, for us God's love makes it simple enough.

The sacraments are demonstrations of this. They represent our need to draw near to the source of life which is not to be found in ourselves but the One who calls us to Himself, our need to know that this is in fact happening to us and to proclaim it as a public event not only a private experience. Naturally we want to do this as well as we can, bringing all that we treasure in our lives as human beings so that we can lay it all at the feet of the God whom we set out to worship. We bring our own creativity as a gift to the One who gives it to us. The Eucharist in particular celebrates this exchange of gifts which we see as evidence of our participating in the work of God himself. Bringing what we have made, we bring our love for God, just as God in Jesus brings life to the world he loves. Eucharist, above all, is an exchange of love, and the way we demonstrate this is by giving one another gifts. The gifts we ourselves bring, however, are symbolic. Like the Magi, we come bearing tokens of our adoration.

Unfortunately it is very easy for us to see the gift itself and ignore, or simply forget, its significance, so that its value is judged by its appearance. This is particularly the case with regard to the gifts we bring as part of our corporate worship. We want our efforts to be appreciated, not only by God but by other people as well. When our offering represents a great deal of human effort (like a performance of Mozart's *Requiem* or many hours spent cultivating a cottage garden), the danger of its actual value becoming distorted is proportionately greater. This is something of which the Old Testament prophets were very much aware, as of course was Jesus himself. The significance of the widow's offering (Mk 1:42; Lk 21:2) lies in its sincere simplicity; here was something which could never be accused of having been 'done for effect.' The same principle applies to corporate worship.

Jesus said, 'Where two or three are gathered together in my name, I am there among them' (Mk 18:20). We should be careful not to confuse numbers with belonging. Where love is exchanged between two people, there is human identity; where more than two are involved, identity becomes belonging. Our most profound experiences begin with encounters *between* before spreading outwards to work *among*. The number of people is what psychologists describe as an epi-phenomenon, not the thing itself, which remains a small-scale event, perhaps the smallest one which ever takes place involving people. It is on this original encounter that our personhood depends, as this is our only chance of knowing other people and being known by them, in other words, of belonging with them.

When we really know someone, in the moment of meeting our personhood is affirmed in the act of acknowledging theirs. As it is with another person, so it is with God; in whatever way he makes himself known to us, God greets us on a one-to-one basis. It was for such intimacy that he created us in the first place. To put it in ordinary terms, the ones we use among ourselves in our daily lives, our own personal knowledge of God should serve to convince us that he prefers quality to quantity. The fact that he is known to reveal Himself to many people at the same time on the same occasion is God's business, not ours, and should not be allowed to interfere with, or detract from, the entirely personal, completely private attention which he is giving to *us*; and when he sends us out to tell others how he has dealt with us, what he goes on meaning in our own lives, we are to do this as personally as we know how. This should be our main concern. The nature of the sacrament itself – the One who is all, the few who are many – proclaims the defeat of any statistical approaches.

Personal does not always mean private. All the same, spiritual experience has a degree of intimacy which can make us hesitate to mention it, even if we would like to do so. This is because what is involved here is not something which belongs to a category of things; it is the uniqueness which categories set out to disempower – a unique encounter, so personal as to be practically indescribable, resembling nothing other than itself. This is what you will share with others – not an explanation but a gift to be given away.

Sacrament exists as the place and time of this exchange. It cannot be forced on anyone and remain itself. Once it has been experienced, however, it will never be forgotten, which is why I have called it transformative. It is essentially private and totally shared. In it the humanly personal re-discovers the scope of its own God-given nature, the betweenness which is the birth of belonging:

Love bade me welcome; yet by soul drew back
    Guiltie of dust and sinne
But quick-eye'd Love, observing me grow slack
    From my first entrance in
Drew nearer to me, sweetly questioning,
    If I lack'd anything.

A guest, I answer'd, worthy to be here:
    Love said, you shall be he.
I the unkind, ungrateful! Ah my deare,
    I cannot look on thee.

Love took my hand and smiling did reply,
    Who made the eyes but I?

Truth, Lord, but I have marr'd them! Let my shame
    Go where it doth deserve
And know you not, sayes Love, who bore the blame?
    My deare, then I will serve
You must sit down, says Love, and taste my meat;
    So I did sit and eat.

GEORGE HERBERT

EPILOGUE
(ASCENSION DAY 2011)

'I, when I am lifted up from the earth,
will draw all people to myself'. (Jn 12:32)

At the beginning of this book we considered the way in which human beings experience relationship in the action of reaching out to one another across the distance which divides them, so that instead of simply being individuals they can be seen and known as individuals-in-relation. Indeed they have to experience life in this way in order to grow in personhood. We do not learn to live together by cancelling out the distance which separates us but by using that distance in order to draw closer. For us, meeting and parting belong together: our experience of belonging is one in which contact and separation are bound intimately together and our salvation, the transformation of our lives, is mediated through this interchange. In the story of Jesus, Incarnation and Ascension are revealed at Pentecost as God's assertion of the truth that, for those who believe, nothing is permanently lost even though to possess it we also have to bid it goodbye, as it is only by doing this that we can be included within a belonging which nothing can ever destroy.

> When he was going and they were gazing up to heaven, suddenly two men in white robes stood by them. They said, 'Men of Galilee, why do you stand looking up toward heaven? This Jesus, who has been taken up from you into heaven, will come in the same way as you saw him go into heaven. (Ac 1:10, 11)

The story of what happened both distances us from Christ and draws us to him. It reminds us of the essential terms of our belonging.

For us, from the very beginning of awareness, presence has depended upon absence in order to be itself. Our knowledge of Jesus Christ, like our experience of being human, shows distance and belonging are one . . .

APPENDIX I

During the 11th century, the mediaeval form of the initiation process was systematised in the *ordo baptismi* of the missal of Gelasius II. Those to be baptised were first of all admitted to the initial degree of catechumen. This in itself involved three significant ritual actions: exsufflation with an exorcism formula, signing with the cross on the forehead and anointing with salt that had been previously exorcised. The initiatory nature of this procedure is clear enough: the first action separates, the second both separates and incorporates, the third is a definite rite of incorporation, this purpose being made explicit in an accompanying prayer. Taken together, the three ritual actions comprise the first complete rite of the ritual complex of Christian Baptism. In the degree of the catechumenate men and women are called from their natural state of existence in the profane world, the world corrupted by sin, and are very definitely and systematically separated or set aside for incorporation in the New Creation.

The next stage of initiation, the transitional period, consisted of instruction in, and experience of, Christian doctrine and liturgy. Candidates were allowed to attend worship, but were required to leave before the beginning of the Canon of the Mass. That is, they were not yet in a position to participate in the sacred mysteries but could familiarise themselves with the liturgical setting and benefit from the teaching contained in the Ministry of the Word. During this central section of the rite, each candidate underwent a series of exorcisms to separate him or her more and more completely from the non-Christian world. This part of the rite symbolised a time of change, in which initiates were kept very much in an in-between state, no longer permitted to enjoy the freedoms and indulgences of 'the world' and not yet admitted to the richer and more permanent joys of belonging to Christ's own family. The central section of the ritual complex was brought to a close by the actions which comprised the *effeta*. This final ceremony of the central phase took place in three parts: firstly, the priest moistened his finger with saliva and touched the top part of each candidate's upper lip; secondly, candidates undressed and were anointed on the chests and backs with consecrated oil; thirdly, they renounced Satan, committed themselves to Christ and recited the Credo. Thus, this second stage in the initiatory complex, like the first, contains rites that separate and prepare for incorporation. However, its main character is transitional, for it is a time of painful growth in which the initiand finds him or herself shaken free from the ties of the world without having yet attained to a position in which he or she can set foot on the firm rock and march boldly forward as a 'soldier of Christ.' At the same time, the seeds of new life are being planted and the ideas of impregnation and conception are suggested by the *effeta* as a symbolic way of preparing for the birth which is to follow.

The post-liminal section of the three-fold ritual complex was the Baptism itself. The action of sprinkling each individual catechumen with consecrated water constituted the pre-liminal movement of this section, standing as a symbol of separation and consecration. However it was also the keynote of the final phase of the completed complex and this gave it the force of post-liminality, making it a powerful symbol of initiation-as-incorporation, the celebration of an event which has been finally completed, in this case a transformation of individual being now perfectly achieved. The two successive stages of this final section confirm this understanding. In the central section, the newly baptised, having been assisted by their godmothers and godfathers to dress themselves in white garments, are brought before the bishop to be marked with the sign of the cross, emblem par excellence of liminal suffering and post-liminal triumph. Finally, the new Christians received their special beverage of milk, honey and water – food suitable for the infants of the New Creation – and having been Confirmed, shared in the Mass.

In fact, however, by Gelasius time, the growth of the practice of infant baptism had necessitated a radical re-arrangement of this order. The pre-liminal stage of entry into the catechumenate and the liminal experiences of the catechumens themselves became detached from the ceremonies associated with baptism proper and transferred to a later stage of Christian initiation, the Sacrament of Confirmation. At the same time the three-fold rite of baptism itself, the final phase of the early mediaeval initiatory complex, was adjusted to take account of the fact that the neophytes could no longer 'speak for themselves,' so that the actions of renouncing Satan and promising allegiance to Christ must be performed on their behalf by the godparents. These gestures now constitute the pre-liminal phase of Holy Baptism, along with the action of blessing the water, for they represent the church's initial movement of readiness to receive a new member. Thus the baptism returns to its most significant place, as a liminal or pivoting moment symbolising a crucial change from death to life which is the crux of the sacramental action. The signing of the cross is the seal of new membership of the Body of Christ, and this is accompanied by actions which express the reality of Christian belonging (for instance, the lighting of candles to represent illumination by the 'Light of the World') and the church's joy at receiving the neophyte, some of which are performed by the godparents as representatives of the welcoming Christian community.

APPENDIX II
(SILENT WORSHIP)

I am sitting next to Evelyn, in the choir stalls of the hospital chapel. Evelyn, who has been a patient in this hospital for at least twenty-five of her fifty years, is singing away lustily with the rest of us. But the words she is singing are quite different from the ones I am singing myself. So different in fact that I can hardly make them out at all. But it does not matter, 'God is his own interpreter, And He will make it plain,' the rest of us sing.

In *Religious Thinking from Childhood to Adolescence* Goldman says that 'some religious experiences are so profound and personal and mysterious that it is doubtful if they are communicable at all, except through the emotional language of the arts.' In Evelyn's case, it is simple enough. She is not able to read. She is simply feeling religious emotions and singing religious words in a religious way. The result is, she sounds just like the six-year-old child quoted by Goldman:

> Thy deliberately Faith I fill,
> Faith against almighty worship God,
> And Faith all unto you,
> Faith against thy holy prayer.

But, in fact, communication with Evelyn, in the setting of corporate worship, is not difficult. Not at the level of Christian fellowship. It would be difficult to discuss the relative merits of the Antiochene and Alexandrian doctrines of Incarnation with her or to consider together the ways in which Augustine's understanding of the atonement differs from the view held by Irenaeus. It would be almost impossible to make the doctrine of the Eucharist clear from a philosophical point of view. But to taste and see the substance of God's glory, to share the real presence of Divinity – that is very easy. And because it is easy, it is good. To worship with Evelyn is a gracious communion. In the action of sharing in this way, at this time, in this place, we are made one in the unity of Christ. Here, in the Eucharist, communication is a common awareness which is non-discursive. A communion in which the 'prevailing presence' is allowed to 'be his own interpreter'. Despite the difference in our ways of organising our thoughts, we are in communion with one another, and with God. And indeed, our communion is the resolution of all differences, the answer to all arguments, the completion of every epistomological position throughout the entire hospital. For in the place and time of our symbolic sharing we are welcomed into a kind of disclosure which transcends the propositional. as love transcends ambivalence, or as *agape* overcomes, includes and transforms *eros*. This is communication received and experienced not as transmission of concepts but as inspiriting event. Communication as the relationship.

Here in church, whether the church is improvised or 'purpose-built', the wards or the huge Victorian-Gothic chapel, there takes place an acted parable of the triumph of the embodied-personal over the intellectual-inclusionist. Although this is hard to put down in words it is something with which as Christians we are familiar enough. Perhaps because we are too familiar with it, it needs stating over and over again. In our Eucharists we supersede ideas and formulae, and the inevitable human tendency for ideas to end up as formulae. Here, in the psychiatric hospital, the truth is blessedly apparent. It is a truth which needs no words, and one which no words can obscure. Here our liturgy escapes from our obsessional attempts to express ourselves in ways which cannot possibly be misunderstood, an attempt which has led us into an endless aggregation of words – descriptive words, exegetical discourses, arguments, explanations, exhortations – to produce a watertight liturgy, a final statement of God's intention. 'Do this in remembrance of me' – the command stands forth from the page in all its simplicity, confounding our effort to hedge it about with an almost impenetrable forest of verbiage. But it is in situations like this one where so many of those who are gathered together are not able to comprehend the subtleties of our theology that its miraculous straightforwardness is most striking, most amazing. The action speaks for itself: 'Do this.' What we do is share. What we are sharing is God. As with the hymns and prayers, so with the bread and the wine. We already know about this. Now, in obedience to Christ's command, we come forward to know it better. Each in his own way, and all together.

From ROGER GRAINGER, 'Watching for Wings', 1979

NOTES

Chapter I

1 W. R. D. Fairbairn, 'A revised psychopathology of the psychoses and psychoneuroses,' 1941, in *Psychoanalytic Studies of the Personality*, 1952, p. 48.

2 Charles Williams, *Descent into Hell*, 1937, p. 248.

3 Martin Buber, *Between Man and Man*, 1961, p. 204.

4 Paul Tillich, *The Courage to Be*, 1962, ch. iv.

5 B. Major and C. P. Eccleston, 'Stigma and social exclusion' in D. Abrams, M. A. Hogg and J. M. Marquis, *The Social Psychology of Inclusion and Exclusion*, 2005, pp. 63–87. See also Roger Grainger, *Laying the Ghost*, 2009.

6 R. D. Laing, *The Divided Self*, 1959, p. 43.

7 E. Erikson, *The Life-Cycle Completed*, 1985.

8 Cf. Erving Goffman, *The Presentation of Self in Everyday Life*, 1971; also T. J. Scheff, *Goffman Unbound*, 2006.

9 C. Howarth, 'A social representation is not a quiet thing', 2006, *British Journal of Social Psychology*, 45(1), 65–86.

10 S. Kierkegaard, *Crisis in the Life of an Actress* (trans. S. Crites), 1967.

11 Martin Buber, *I and Thou*, 1966.

12 Martin Buber, *Pointing the Way*, 1957, pp. 66, 67–73.

13 Cf. M. Duggan and R. Grainger, *Imagination, Identification and Catharsis in Theatre and Therapy*, 1997; also R. Grainger, *Suspending Disbelief*, 2010.

14 Paul Tillich, *The Dynamics of Faith*, 1957.

15 Karl Jaspers, *The Nature of Psychotherapy*, 1964, p. 6.

16 This is a principal theme of C. J. Jung's psychology. See *Analytical Psychology*, 1968; *Psychology and Religion*, 1938; Jolande Jacobi, *The Psychology of C. G. Jung*, 1942. The importance of religious faith for psychological healing was a life-long pre-occupation for Viktor Frankl, viz. *Psychology and Existentialism*, 1973; *The Unconscious God*, 1977.

17 Rudoph Otto, *The Idea of the Holy*, 1923, p. 25.

Chapter II

18 Richard Lovelace, 1618–1658.
19 Cf. D. P. McAdams *The Stories We Live By*, 1993; S. Corrie and D. A. Lane, *Constructing Stories and Telling Tales* (Karnac Books), 2010.
20 Martin Buber, *I and Thou*, 1966, pp. 9, 11.
21 Cf. R. Grainger, *Suspending Disbelief*, 2010.
22 Alida Gersie, 1992, pp. 19, 29.
23 T. S. Eliot, 'The Journey of the Magi'; cf. also G. W. Stroup, *The Promise of Narrative Theology*, 1981.

Chapter III

24 See J. C. Gunzberg, *Healing Through Meeting: Martin Buber's Conversational Approach to Psychotherapy*, 1997.
25 See M. Buber, *Between Man and Man*, 1961.
26 H. Hubert and M. Mauss, *Mélanges d'Histoire des Réligions*, 1909, p. 190.
27 A. Van Gennep, *The Rites of Passage*, 1960.
28 B. Malinowski, *Magic, Science and Religion*, 1974.
29 V. Turner, *The Ritual Process*, 1974.
30 Ibid., pp. 70, 71, 81.
31 C. Gorman, *The Book of Ceremony*, 1972 p. 45.
32 Jacqueline Akhurst, 'Exploring the Nexus between Wilderness and Therapeutic Experiences', *Implicit Religion*, 13(3): 2010, pp. 295–305, 301, 304.
33 A. P. Elkin, *Aboriginal Man of High Degree*, 1946.
34 M. Eliade, *Rites and Symbols of Initiation*, 1965 p. 128.

Chapter IV

35 M. Eliade, *The Sacred and the Profane*, 1959. Eliade wrote extensively on the subject. See *Patterns in Comparative Religion*, 1958. Much of what has been written on this subject is derived from the work of Jane Harrison, *Themis*, 1963.
36 M. Eliade, *The Sacred and the Profane*,1959, p. 26.
37 S. Pendjik, 1992 – an extract from a paper delivered at the British Association of Drama Therapists Conference, September 1992.
38 C. Gorman, *op. cit.*, p. 45.
39 D. Langley, *An Introduction to Dramatherapy*, 2006. Langley goes into this question at greater depth.
40 M. Buber, *Pointing the Way*, 1957, p. 66. See also M. Duggan and R. Grainger, *Imagination, Identification and Catharsis in Theatre and Therapy,* 1997, p. 65.

41 S. Kierkegaard, *Crisis in the Life of an Actress*, 1967, p. 87.

42 P. Brook, *The Empty Space*, 1968.

43 S. T. Coleridge, *Biographia Literaria*, 1817. See also R. Grainger, *Suspending Disbelief*, 2010.

44 N. Broadbent, personal communication. Neil Broadbent is the Director of *Sozein*, a centre of Christian healing based near Derby.

Chapter V

45 A. Van Gennep, *The Rites of Passage*, 1960.

46 Cf. G. Lewis, *The Day of Shining Red*, 1980.

47 A. Van Gennep, op. cit., p. 10.

48 Cf. R. Grainger, *The Message of the Rite*, 1988.

49 Cf R. Grainger, *The Drama of the Rite*, 2009.

50 J-Y Hameline, 'Les Rites de Passage', *Maison-Dieu* 112, 1972, pp. 133–144.

Chapter VI

51 A. Van Gennep, *The Rites of Passage*, 1960, p. 189.

52 Cf. P. Ricœur, *The Rule of Metaphor: Multi-Disciplinary Studies of the Creation of Meaning in Language*, 1978 (translation by Robert Czerny of *La Metaphore Vive*).

53 Cf. R. Grainger, *The Language of the Rite*, 1974; *Staging Posts*, 1987.

54 Cf. R. Grainger, 1974.

55 Cf. M. Elaide, *Rites and Symbols of Initiation*, 1965.

56 As the final human rite of passage, funeral rituals throughout the world reproduce tis therapeutic action in a way which is particularly striking. See R. Grainger, *The Unburied*, 1988; *The Social Symbolism of Grief and Mourning*, 1998.

57 R. Aechtner, 2010.

Chapter VII

58 From the Collect for the Second Sunday of Epiphany, *Common Worship*, 2000, p. 384.

59 Cf. R. Grainger, *The Drama of the Rite*, 2009.

60 Ibid., pp. 1–4.

61 F. W. Dillistone, 'The Function of Symbols in Religious Experience' in ed. Dillistone *Myth and Symbol*, 1966.

Chapter VIII

62 Cf. R. Grainger, *The Message of the Rite,* 1988.

63 See D. Abrams, M. A. Hogg and J. M. Margues, *The Social Symbolism of Inclusion and Exclusion*, 2005.

64 'To the extent that one's productivity, one's products, one's self come under the control of others, they become alien to him', R. Schacht, *Alienation*, 1971 p. 260.

65 See Appendix, V. Turner, *The Ritual Process*, 1974.

66 Cf. Lewis Bouyer, *Rite and Man*, 1963.

Chapter IX

67 H. McCabe, *The New Creation*, 1969, p. 62.

68 *Henry V*, Chorus.

69 Richard of St Victor, 'The Trinity' in *The Twelve Patriarchs*, 1979.

70 See Emile Mersch, *The Whole Christ*, 1962 (Translation by J. R. Kelly of *Le Corps Mystique Du Christ*, 1936).

71 H. Cox, *The Secular City*, 1965.

72 L. S. Thornton, *The Common Life in the Body of Christ*, 1942.

Chapter X

73 E. I. Bailey, *Implicit Religion in Contemporary Society*, 1997; *The Secular Faith Controversy*, 2001.

74 See Appendix II.

BIBLIOGRAPHY

Abrams, D., Marques, J. and Hogg, M. A. (eds.) (2004), *The Social Psychology of Inclusion and Exclusion,* Hove: Psychology Press.

Aechtner, R. (2010), Jugendfeier: *A secular humanist youth rite of passage ritual,* Denton Conference, Ilkley, UK.

Akhurst, J. (2010), Exploring the nexus between wilderness and therapeutic experiences, *Implicit Religion* 13(3), pp. 295–305.

Bailey, E. I. (1997), *Implicit Religion in Contemporary Society,* Kampen NL: Kok Pharos.

Bailey, E. I. (2001), *The Secular Faith Controversy,* London: Continuum.

Bouyer, L. (1963), *Rite and Man,* London: Burns & Oates.

Brook, P. (1968), *The Empty Space,* London: MacGibbon & Kee.

Buber, M. (1957), *Pointing the Way,* London:| Routledge & Kegan Paul.

Buber, M. (1961), *Between Man and Man,* London: Collins.

Buber, M. (1970), *I and Thou,* Edinburgh: Clark.

Coleridge, S. T. (1817), *Biographia Literaria,* 2 vols, London: Rest Fenner.

Corrie, S. and Lane, D. (2010), *Constructing Stories, Telling Tales,* London: Karnac.

Cox, H. G. (1965), *The Secular City,* London: SCM Press.

Dillistone, F. W. (1966), The function of symbols in religious experience in F. W. Dillistone (ed.), *Myth and Symbol,* London: SPCK.

Duggan, M. and Grainger, R. (1997), *Imagination, Identification and Catharsis in Theatre and Therapy,* London: Jessica Kingsley.

Eliade, M. (1965), *Rites and Symbols of Initiation,* New York: Harper & Row.

Eliade, M. (1958), *Patterns in Comparative Religion,* London: Sheed and Ward.

Eliade, M. (1959), *The Sacred and the Profane,* New York: Harcourt Brace.

Elkin, A. P. (1945), *Aboriginal Men of High Degree . . . ,* Sydney: Australasian Publishing Company.

Erikson E. H. (1983), *Life Cycle Completed,* London: W. W. Norton.

Fairbairn, R. W. (1952), *Psychoanalytic Studies of the Personality,* London: Routledge & Kegan Paul.

Frankl, V. E. (1973), *Psychotherapy and Existentialism,* Harmondsworth: Penguin.

Frankl, V. E. (1977), *The Unconscious God*, London: Hodder and Stoughton.

Gersie, A. (1992), *Earthtales: Storytelling in Times of Change*, London: Green Print.

Goffman, E. (1971), *The Presentation of Self in Everyday Life*, Harmondsworth: Penguin.

Gorman, C. (1972), *The Book of Ceremony*, Cambridge: Whole Earth Tools.

Grainger, R. (1974), *The Language of the Rite*, London: Darton Longman and Todd.

Grainger, R. (1988), *The Message of the Rite*, Cambridge: Lutterworth.

Grainger, R (1988), *The Unburied*, Worthing: Churchman.

Grainger, R (1998), *The Social Symbolism of Grief and Mourning*, London: Jessica Kingsley.

Grainger, R (2009), *The Drama of the Rite*, Brighton, Portland, Toronto: Sussex Academic Press.

Grainger, R. (2009), *Laying the Ghost*, London: Chipmunka.

Grainger, R. (2010), *Suspending Disbelief*, Brighton, Portland, Toronto: Sussex Academic Press.

Gunzburg, J. C. (1997), *Healing through Meeting*, London: Jessica Kingsley.

Hameline, J.-Y. (1972), Les rites de passage, *Maison-Dieu*, pp. 112, 133–144.

Harrison, J. E. (1963), *Themis*, 2nd ed., London: Merlin Press.

Howarth, C. (2006), A social representation is not a quiet thing: exploring the critical potential of social representations theory, *British Journal of Social Psychology* 45(1), 65–86.

Hubert, H. and Mauss, M. (1909), *Mélanges d'histoire des réligions*, Paris: Alkan.

Jacobi, J. (1942), *The Psychology of C. G. Jung*, London: Kegan Paul.

Jaspers, K (1964), *The Nature of Psychotherapy*, Manchester: Manchester University Press.

Jung, C. G. (1938), *Psychology and Religion*, New Haven, CT: Yale University Press.

Jung, C. G. (1968), *Analytical Psychology*, London: Routledge & Kegan Paul.

Kierkegaard, S. (1967), *Crisis in the Life of an Actress, and other essays on drama* (translated by S. Crites), London: Collins.

Laing, R. D. (1960), *The Divided Self*, London: Tavistock.

Langley, D. M. (2006), *An Introduction to Dramatherapy*, London: Sage.

Lewis, G. (1980), *Day of Shining Red*, Cambridge: Cambridge University Press.

Major, B. and Eccleston, C. P. (2004), Stigma and social exclusion in D. Abrams, J. Marques, and M. A. Hogg, *The Social Psychology of Inclusion and Exclusion*, Hove: Psychology Press.

Malinowski, B. (1974), *Magic, Science and Religion,* London: Souvenir.

McAdams, D. P. (1993), *The Stories We Live By*, New York: Guilford.

McCabe, H. (1964), *The New Creation*, London: Sheed & Ward.

Mersch, E. (1938), *The Whole Christ*, London: Dobson.

Otto, R (1924), *The Idea of the Holy*, Oxford: Oxford University Press.

Ricœur, P. (1978), *The Rule of Metaphor* (translation by R. Czerny of *La méta-phore vive*), London: Routledge & Kegan Paul.

Schacht, R. (1971), *Alienation* London: Allen & Unwin.

Scheff, T. J. (2006), *Goffman Unbound!*, Boulder, CO: Paradigm.

Stroup, G. W. (1981), *The Promise of Narrative Theology*, London: SCM Press.

St Victor, Richard of (1979), *The Twelve Patriarchs; The Mystical Ark; Book Three of the Trinity*, New York: Paulist Press.

Thornton, L. S. (1941), *The Common Life in the Body of Christ*, London: Dacre Press.

Tillich, P. (1957), *The Dynamics of Faith*, New York: Harper & Bros.

Tillich, P. (1962), *The Courage to Be*, London: Collins.

Turner, V. W. (1974), *The Ritual Process*, Harmondsworth: Penguin.

Van Gennep, A. (1960), *The Rites of Passage*, London: Routledge & Kegan Paul.

Williams, C. (1937), *Descent into Hell*, London: Faber & Faber.

INDEX